GRACE BULGER
is a marketing consultant who
specializes in corporate identity work.
The former vice president of communications
for GE Capital Rail Services, she has also
studied a variety of spiritual disciplines for many
years. Bulger lives in Chicago, Illinois.

The ENLIGHTENED *Entrepreneur*

The ENLIGHTENED Entrepreneur

A Spiritual Approach to Creating and Marketing a Company

Grace Bulger

MARLOWE & COMPANY
NEW YORK

The Enlightened Entrepreneur:
A Spiritual Approach to Creating and Marketing a Company
Copyright © 2002 by Grace Bulger

Published by
Marlowe & Company
An Imprint of Avalon Publishing Group Incorporated
161 William Street, 16th Floor
New York, NY 10038

All rights reserved. No part of this book may be reproduced in whole or in part without written permission from the publisher, except by reviewers who may quote brief excerpts in connection with a review in a newspaper, magazine, or electronic publication; nor may any part of this book be reproduced, stored in a retrieval system, or transmitted in any form or by any means electronic, mechanical, photocopying, recording, or other, without written permission from the publisher.

Library of Congress Cataloging-in-Publication Data
is available for this title.
ISBN 1-56924-544-4

9 8 7 6 5 4 3 2 1

Designed by Pauline Neuwirth, Neuwirth & Associates, Inc.

Distributed by Publishers Group West
Printed in the United States of America

Dedicated to my parents,
Roger and Ruth Bulger.

Contents

Introduction 1

One
KEEPING IT REAL 7

Two
PURSUING JOY 25

Three
CLIMBING THE RIGHT MOUNTAIN 37

Four
FULFILLING YOUR PURPOSE 55

Five
ENVISIONING THE POSSIBILITIES 73

Six
LEADING WITH VALUES 87

Seven
TELLING TALES FROM THE HEART 105

Eight
CONNECTING WITH YOUR AUDIENCE 119

Nine
REACHING YOUR GOALS 143

Ten
BUILDING A COMMUNITY 161

Eleven
FACING THE ABYSS 175

Twelve
KEEPING THE FAITH 191

Enlightening Material 203

Acknowledgments 207

Select Associates and Clients 209

The ENLIGHTENED *Entrepreneur*

INTRODUCTION

IF YOUR DREAM is to start your own company, then let's be clear about it: you're doing more than just incorporating a business related to what you do or physicalizing an outgrowth of your personality. You are giving birth to a living entity, with a spirit and soul and personality. This is a sacred creative act that demands respect. This book takes you through a process to help you create and market your own company as clearly and consciously as possible.

As a marketing consultant, I have had the opportunity to help numerous clients in a variety of industries create and market organizations that reflect their values and help them reach their goals. After many rewarding years in marketing, corporate and internal communications, I left to start my own company so that I could live the kind of life I wanted, with the freedom to work with a diverse group of clients, while also pursuing my other passions and creative pursuits. Since that time, I've spent several years helping others do the same thing—and have learned a great deal in the process.

I wrote this book to share with you what I have learned. *The Enlightened Entrepreneur* is not just about how to develop a new business but how to create a company that expresses who you are, brings you fulfillment, and helps you achieve your life's mission.

Marketing Is an Expression of Your Company's Spirit

A FEW YEARS ago, my parents gave me a simple, handmade doll made by a woman in Charleston, South Carolina. The doll's face is basically a round wooden ball, with crudely painted eyes, eyelashes, and a mouth in the shape of a U. She wears a turban and billowy dress of green, purple, yellow, and orange material, with lace trimming and a little gold fabric necklace. Under the dress, her body is a stick surrounded by a bag of potpourri. She carries a little basket of chinaberries in her fabric arms. The doll is a depiction of the women who used to sell flowers on the street corners of Charleston, wearing large skirts to hide their wares.

When I first saw this doll, I fell in love with her inexplicably and immediately. I put her on a high shelf in my bedroom, where my cats can't get her and from which she smiles sweetly at me every morning. Something about her is just—special.

On my next trip to Charleston, I asked my parents where I could buy another of these dolls. They took me to a booth in the open-air market downtown, where I first met Dorothy, who was every bit as sweet as my doll. Fifteen or so dolls, each with their name written on a paper tag, were set up on a little makeshift shelf. Each one was simple and unique. I bought a couple more dolls as gifts, carefully selecting the perfect one for each friend.

After I picked them out, Dorothy took me to the back of the booth and asked me where I was taking them. I told her, and she carefully wrote "Carlotta—Chicago" and "Clara—Chicago" in the notebook. "I like to know where my babies go," she explained. "Look, one of them went to the Dominican Republic yesterday!"

She went on to explain how she had five hundred names, so each doll would have her own name, along with her own unique dress. She explained why she chose the specific trim to go with the fabric of Clara's dress, and showed me a little detail I had missed on Carlotta. When I told her I had one of her dolls at home, she asked, "Which one?" I had to admit that I had ripped off the paper tag of the doll I had been given and—horror upon horrors—had actually forgotten her name! (I felt unbelievably guilty.) "But I love her!" I said. Dorothy smiled forgivingly and said, "I can tell."

Before I gave my friends the dolls I bought for them, I actually thought through whether or not they would care about the dolls as much as they should, and what I would do if they didn't. Falling back on my corporate background, I developed an "exit plan" for little Carlotta and Clara. Fortunately, I didn't have to execute it because both of my friends were as taken with these simple little dolls as I was, giving them prime spots in their living room and office, respectively.

Since then, I've brought several friends to Dorothy's booth. Without fail, my friends have been touched and thrilled by these little dolls and have each found their perfect little match (and I've found two more, one my namesake). We are professional women in our thirties! This is not how we typically react to dolls. But Dorothy's magic touched us all.

My reaction—and the reaction of others—to this very simple product is an example of how passion and love can inspire strong emotional reactions in others. Just as each of these dolls carries Dorothy's energy, every product and service has the potential of encapsulating the same type of energy. In my experience, this type of attractive force exists when people are operating from their hearts from the center of their missions, pouring their passion into their company, product, or service. You can feel the energy as soon as you walk in the door . . . through interactions with the people . . . and in the product or service.

My first experience working with this type of essential energy was when I undertook a corporate identity project for a large company in crisis. It had just undergone a major public relations and business crisis, including research that showed that many customers reportedly were afraid of the company's size. The company's survival and ability to grow was threatened. While the facts did not support customers' fears, their perceptions showed the company that they faced some major problems. They needed to figure out who they really were and express that effectively to their customers and the industry at large.

I gathered the leaders of the company together, and then the managers who worked for the leaders, and then the people who did the work. Together, we tried to capture with words what some called the brand, others called the corporate identity, that was actually . . . the spirit of the company.

The spirit. It was there, too, even in a division of a hardcore manufacturing and financial services giant. It had a lot to do with the people who worked there. It had something to do with the people who worked in other divisions, and at the corporate headquarters. It had a little to do with the people who started the company over a century before. But people came and went, and it stayed. It drew some people in and pushed others away. It was molded and shaped and sometimes twisted by the company's shadow, and then rejuvenated by bold acts of genius or integrity. But it was there. And it was spirit. I'm sure of it.

After we captured the spirit as best we could within the company's revamped identity, we began to communicate it to our customers and the industry every way we could. The key was expressing who we were honestly in every interaction. I was amazed at how well people responded. They were seeing the best of who we were, and they could tell somehow that we meant it. We were able to turn perceptions around in a relatively short time, and the company was once again able to grow without our customers' being scared.

Since that time, I've experienced numerous companies as a marketing and communications consultant. As I took on each new assignment—a marketing plan here, a communications campaign there—I first had to work with my clients to capture their companies' identities. Usually, no one else had bothered to answer these simple questions. Who are you? What makes you special? What's your mission? Who are you here to help? Especially in smaller businesses, the answers to those questions evoked amazingly personal and emotional responses from people.

I saw that, in some cases, in certain companies, people were putting their hearts and souls into their work. They were energized; they were healing; they were helping others. At times, transformation, even magic, occurred. If I could tap into that essence and help them express it, the results could be remarkable.

Suddenly, marketing started looking beautiful, like art. I started to realize that marketing can be downright spiritual. At its highest, it is the expression of a company's spirit.

I've long felt that my job as a marketing consultant focusing on brand and identity is to tap into the best part of each company—its spirit—and find ways to express it honestly and effectively to the world at large. My motto is that marketing at its highest is an expression of a company's essence, those elements that set it apart from its competitors, distinguish its products and services, attract clients, and motivate its employees to get out of bed in the morning.

Of course, along the way, I've seen countless examples of how tapping into a company's spirit makes great things happen. You can motivate and inspire employees . . . magnetically attract the right customers and partners . . . stimulate interest and business . . . and positively impact the world around you. In fact, you can actually see the company begin operating on a higher level of integrity, and becoming a stronger, more beneficial force. You can actually make the company better.

I also realized that focusing on a company's identity from its inception can be an extremely useful process. Conscious creation is in many ways preferable to what usually occurs, which is the company develops and the personality emerges, sometimes overtaking the spirit of the company. I began to work with people who were just setting out on the journey of creating their own company, enabling me to help facilitate the identity and marketing process from the beginning. And I realized that the beginning was way before I thought. . . . It was more fundamental even than the idea for the business. It started with the person or people creating the company. That's how my approach expanded to encompass more than just marketing.

Embracing the Task Ahead

THIS BOOK IS designed to take you through this process and to help you create your company within a philosophical context. It will help you develop not only your company's identity and overall marketing and marketing communications strategy, but also a clearer understanding of how your company can fit into your life and help you achieve your personal mission and vision.

Each chapter focuses on one major principle for consciously creating your company. The principles are:

1. Be authentic.
2. Follow your passions.
3. Define success for yourself.
4. Serve others by following your mission.
5. Develop a clear vision.
6. Be true to your values.
7. Tell your story.
8. Adapt your messages to your audience.
9. Develop concrete goals and flexible strategies.
10. Value relationships.

11. Be courageous.
12. Work with the universe.

While individually each principle may be something you've heard before, or self-evident, taken together they constitute for me an essential, unique route to becoming an enlightened entrepreneur.

To help you on your way to entrepreneurial enlightenment, I've organized each chapter into three parts:

- An introductory discussion of the principle
- Your life—the application of the principle to you
- Your company—the application of the principle to your company

Beginning with how the principle can be integrated into your life and then exploring how it relates to your company keeps the focus on designing a company that enhances your life instead of taking it over.

You may find it helpful to read through this book quickly at first, giving your answers without stopping to think too hard, and then going back through a second time more thoughtfully to fill in areas you may have missed. I recommend keeping a journal or notebook in which to record your answers, as it will be an essential companion as you read the book, which includes many questions to answer and a number of exercises that build on each other along the journey.

If you are starting your company with one or more partners, taking time to complete this fundamental step of the process becomes even more crucial. It allows you all to be aware of each other's explicit goals, values, and issues. I've found it to be helpful if partners first answer these questions individually, share their answers with each other, and then answer the questions again together, from the perspective of their partnership. Your strengths as an individual may be very different than the strengths of your partnership, for example. And it can't ever hurt to compare and discuss your issues and challenges, individually and together.

While *The Enlightened Entrepreneur* is not the only source of information you'll need as you set out on the entrepreneurial path, it will help you develop a context in which to consciously create your company to work for you.

One

Keeping It Real

1. be authentic

The process of developing your company starts with you—with who you are. If you come up with a way to fill one of your own needs or desires, you may well find that many others feel the same way.

Creating a company is living art. It is a way of expressing yourself in the physical world, focusing and expanding your energy to serve yourself and others. As the founder and leader of your company, you are giving birth to a new, living entity. With your intentions and your energy, you are shaping your company in a lasting way. The more honest and self-aware you are—about who you are, your gifts and talents, your issues and challenges—the more conscious you can be about developing the clearest, highest possible manifestation of your company.

Some ideas are lemonade stands. Some ideas are multinational corporations. Trying to make an idea that is meant to be a lemonade stand into a multinational corporation may not be the best idea. Some ideas have a short life, and that's as it should be. Maybe they are a stepping-stone to somewhere else. Other ideas could last for decades. It's up to you and the universe. All you can really do is trust, listen to yourself and remain true to who you are.

IN HIS BOOK, *The Tom Peters Seminar: Crazy Times Call for Crazy Organizations*, Tom Peters posits, "Companies listen too much to their customers." Peters says, "Almost all the world's progress comes from people who have it their own way," and he gives several examples:

- **Chuck Williams of Williams Sonoma says he just bought what he liked.**
- **Sigeru Miyamoto, creator of Nintendo's Super Mario game, says, "The game is not for children, it is for me."**
- **Architect Christopher Day says, "Unless I can design something nourishing to my soul—nourishing, not just nice, dramatic, photogenic, novel—I can't expect it to be nourishing to anyone else."**

Be Yourself

WE ALL HAVE something unique and important to offer the world. If we try to deny who we are, we ignore and dishonor our individuality—and no one else can fill that void. When we honor who we are, we can inspire and serve others.

Ella Leya, once a famous singer in Russia, experienced great difficulty establishing a career in the United States. She grew up Jewish in predominantly Muslim Azerbaijan, was trained as a classical musician, and spent several years in Moscow as a musical and theater star, singing American jazz. As you might imagine, her style is eclectic, to say the least. Although many people in the American music industry were supportive of her talent, they did not know what box to put her in. Initially, she tried to adapt her music to fit within existing genres, but it never felt right.

Instead of giving in, Ella created her own record label, B-Elite Records, out of her new home in Chicago. She searched far and wide for a producer who would share her vision, and finally found a producer in L.A. who supported her unique style.

Together, they created an album of major studio quality that perfectly expressed her vision and approach. Ella says, "I blend so many different cultural and ethnic instruments that I could never fit into an existing label. But not everyone has the same cute nose. I want people to hear how different you can be, and I want to help expand the narrow definitions of current genres."

Through her label, she initially distributed and promoted her album herself, learning the ropes of the industry. It was baptism by fire, but she generated extensive publicity, has been performing regularly in attractive venues, and her CDs are flying off the shelves in her targeted cities, especially given that she has done it all herself. She now plans to include other musicians on her label, using her newfound industry knowledge to help them. "I'm here to deliver a message through my music, to inspire people to find something different about themselves," she says. "And there are plenty of great musicians all over the world who combine different types of music and can't fit into a box. I created my record label to allow me to be everything I am, and now I can help other musicians who cross genre and language and culture share their work with the world."

When I tell people Ella's story, they often say, "I'd love to do something like that when I have enough money." We feel like we have to wait to do what we love, but the fact is that Ella created her label on a shoestring budget. It's not about having the money first. It's about doing what you love.

It sure worked for Ella, who has been capturing national attention, all through her own initiative.

Listen to Your Intuition

We know when we're not doing what's right for us. We feel it. We hear that inner voice that knows when we are doing "the wrong thing," that begs, pleads, cajoles us to do something more meaningful. And many of us still resist, choosing to stay in less satisfying jobs because we are comfortable and afraid. Lots of people hold jobs that no longer fit—or never did. Some get sick. Some get depressed. Others (the lucky ones) get fired. It all means the same thing; there's something better for us to do.

Many of my clients initially resisted their inner voices, often when it comes to starting their own companies. We have an idea of what an entrepreneur is supposed to be like, or what we think our life is supposed to be like, and it's hard to let go of that. But that voice persists.

All we have to do is ask for guidance and then really listen.

Lisa Holmes, the founder and artistic director of Whimsy City, a nonprofit theater experience for inner-city children in Chicago, received her inspiration in response to a simple question. She said, "I had been meditating, praying . . . feeling torn between writing for theater or film. I was also feeling sorry for myself because I didn't have the advantages of some of my peers who had great connections and networking opportunities through their Ivy League schools. So I cleared my head, entered a meditative, prayerful state, and asked God and the universe where I should place my focus.

"I asked with the best of intentions, never expecting to hear anything back, I mean, literally hear words ringing in my head. But to my surprise, a message came booming, 'Start a children's theater program on the Southwest side of Chicago.'

"'Huh?' I queried, 'Maybe you didn't hear me correctly. I asked about screenwriting or playwriting. Those are the two choices, now which is it, A or B?'

'Children's theater program' was the final answer. I guess it's no use to argue when a Higher Power is concerned."

Often, people push away what their intuition is telling them because it doesn't match their training or experience. Many of my clients tell me their intuition had been whispering (and, in some cases, screaming) to them for years before they actually made the change.

Jen Shiman, founder and principal of Angry Alien Productions, says, "After years of immersing myself in research and theory of children's interaction with media, I finally followed my true passion—creating and producing the content that I once examined so carefully under the academic microscope. Furthermore, I decided to generate the income I needed through art-based services, such as graphic design and illustration. This direction contrasted wildly with my formal education in international business and media studies. My intuition told me, however, that prioritizing my ongoing love of cartooning and animation would ensure my soul's peace. And I finally listened."

The answers are there for all of us, if we are willing to listen.

Your Life

ANOTHER REASON FOR looking honestly at yourself is this: your company will be in many ways a reflection of you, potentially in both positive and negative ways, so it's best to be conscious right from the start about who you are and what you are doing.

I always used to begin working with aspiring entrepreneurs by helping them to capture their corporate identities, including the company's mission and vision. Over time, and especially with smaller companies or entrepreneurs just starting out, I began to realize that we were missing a crucial piece and that somehow we weren't as anchored or grounded as we could be. I realized how often we ended up discussing the client's personal hopes and dreams as a necessary step in creating the company's vision. In response, I've added this all-important step.

Radiate Your Qualities

OFTEN, THE QUALITIES of founders and leaders infuse the entire company. I have seen this time and time again, whether the company is tiny or gigantic. If the CEO is casual, the company tends to be casual in personality and feeling. If the CEO is nurturing, the company tends to be nurturing. The obvious personality characteristics tend to play themselves out in fascinating ways throughout organizations.

As an employee at GE for many years, I saw how CEO Jack Welch's passion, integrity and drive radiated out and lit up the company, even in some surprising nooks and crannies, like little plants in the middle of small towns far from corporate headquarters. I have worked with many other large companies and found this to be true to varying degrees depending on the passion and spirit of the person at the helm.

In smaller organizations, the impact is even more direct. Cyndi Simon from The Encore Group, Inc., is a friendly, warm, stylish woman from Texas. Everything about her company is friendly, warm, and stylish. I've watched her company grow tremendously, and I've seen several employees come and go over the few years I've worked with her, yet the essence of the company stays the same. Every time I walk through those doors or deal with any member of that company, my experience is consistent. From the decor and dishes to transactions and interpersonal interactions, her personality is reflected.

What are you like? How would you describe yourself? What qualities or characteristics do you possess? How would a friend who knows you well describe you? Include good and bad, and don't be modest.

Take Stock of Your Talents

A TALENT IS something for which you have a natural affinity, regardless of whether or not you've been trained and developed it into a skill. You may have a talent for photography, although you've never taken a class. You may have a talent for languages, although you may or may not have developed fluencies.

It's a good idea to take stock of your talents, because you never know when they may come in handy. It's also helpful when working with partners or hiring employees to have a good idea of what areas you do well so you can build your organization with people with complementary abilities.

A talent can be even more important than a skill, in some cases. When Ella Leya began to sell her first album, she could not afford to hire an outside PR person. She has a remarkable talent for charming her way past closed doors and into people's hearts, however, that proved to be more important. I watched in amazement as she broke every rule and managed to get herself into every Chicago newspaper and onto every radio show she targeted, while developing real friendships with editors, producers and deejays along the way. It was amazing. I had to rethink everything I thought I knew about PR. Now when she asks me for PR advice, I offer some thoughts and basic information but then respectfully tell her to go with her instincts. They've certainly served her well so far.

What are you naturally good at? What talents were you seemingly born with? What comes to you easily and effortlessly?

How can you use these talents in your new company?

Identify Your Skills

YOU MAY NOT realize how many skills you have. Some of them may prove to be unexpectedly useful, and, again, looking at your resources may help you determine which areas you may need to beef up as you start your company.

This is especially helpful when you have partners or employees. One client sent his brochures and annual report out to a high-priced firm to be translated into Italian, only to discover that one of his long-term employees spoke and wrote it fluently. Know what resources are available to you! It could save you money and time.

In what areas do you have technical aptitude?

What skills have you mastered? This could include anything from computer skills to interpersonal skills to interior design.

Be Conscious of Your Issues

Because you are the creator of your company, your issues will be played out and echoed throughout your company also.

In my consulting work, I get a close look at many different companies and their owners and leaders. The leaders' issues become the companies' issues. Leaders who are addicted to crises run companies that are constantly putting out fires. Leaders who can't say no overextend their people and their resources. It's just a fact of business.

Here are some of the major issues of leaders that I have often seen played out in their organizations, large and small.

The Perfectionist

I once worked for the CEO of a division of a large company who gave many presentations to customers, and was also frequently required to present reviews, plans, and budgets to the corporate office that oversaw all the divisions. The leaders of the company took these "pitches" very seriously, and, although the many presentations were scheduled in advance for the entire year, we usually ended up working on them down to the wire.

The CEO of my division was brilliant, creative, ambitious, and a total perfectionist. He always wanted to not only meet his bosses' expectations but to blow them away—and all the other divisions out of the water. And he almost always succeeded.

With every presentation, he would go into "pitch mode." This greatly affected me, his communications person, and my people, as well as many of his other executives and their people, who were often required to generate huge amounts of information. It is no exaggeration to say that a single pitch might significantly impact 20 or 30 people in the division.

Every pitch seemed more painful than the last, with rewrites and revisions and tweaks and disasters occurring up until the very last moment. And then there were the impossible requests—the last-minute videos, the search for photos, the creation of graphics, all to add the extra bang for the buck. I grew to hate the sight of that flashing light on my phone, the sound of his kind, apologetic voice saying, "Hey,

Grace—I had a thought . . . Is it possible to . . ." This is when I learned that almost anything is possible if you have enough money. Brochure by Tuesday? OK. Video by Thursday? Sure. Laser show? No problem! Fork over your wallet and you can have pretty much anything.

As each pitch was completed, you could almost feel the entire office breathe a collective sigh of relief. And we all felt good about what we had done—going for the home run. This pattern became part of the ebb and flow of our work life. We always knew what was coming, and we knew what it was going to cost us. We were trained to work this way, and we began to reflect it in our own management styles, even when it was not directly driven from the top. And who am I kidding? We were all made of the same cloth—ambitious, competitive perfectionists. We wanted it too, or we wouldn't have lasted.

Once I tried to circumvent this process. (Once.) I knew a certain big pitch was coming, and I tried to plan for it in advance. I brainstormed every single piece of information anyone could possibly want. I dragged out every relevant fact, graphic, photograph, and bit of trivia I could think of. I proactively developed an outline of what I thought the CEO would want to address. I even called some people I knew in the relevant departments up at corporate to see if I could get a heads-up on the specifics that were hot that month (or week or day). Then I scheduled a meeting with the CEO, CFO, and other relevant parties to discuss the pitch, a full two weeks before the normal chaos would typically begin.

The meeting was a great success. I walked out with a solid draft of the pitch, complete with buy-in from all involved. As I created the speaker support, I congratulated myself on my new approach. I was still proud two days later as we went through the typical revisions, reversals, and differences of opinions, page by page, word by word. And again two days after that as we revised the pitch again. And two days after that . . . and that weekend . . . and four times the next week. Then, of course, the inevitable information requests came from corporate outlining a totally new approach to the presentation and required information. By the time the pitch (which was stellar as always) actually occurred, I was exhausted, frustrated and guilt-ridden about the veritable forest that had been sacrificed through the eighteen or so drafts we'd generated.

The pattern of behavior was bigger than I was, bigger even than my company (and, many could argue, an unavoidable symptom of the quick pace of business).

It was dug in, unstoppable (at least by me). One thing I could do was to be aware of the pattern and to try and minimize my own part in it, so that I could minimize the impact on my own group. Of course, we all knew that, no matter how well we planned, things can change on a dime.

THE PARANOIAC

Another example of a leader's issues being played out in the organization is this: a client I once worked with was suspicious verging on paranoid. She was convinced that people were always trying to take advantage of her. I was amazed as she cast one person after another in the role of the person who currently was trying to rip her off, and then seemingly created the reality that this was so.

This woman always watched the hours people worked very closely. If someone arrived five minutes late or left five minutes early, she noticed. If someone took a long lunch, she knew. If someone called in sick, she'd call them at home ostensibly to check on their well-being, but really just to see if they were actually home.

At one point, she hired a new office assistant who had to take a train and two buses to the office, which took her an hour and a half each way. In order to arrive by 8:00 A.M., she had to leave by 6:00 A.M. and get to the office at 7:25 A.M. If she missed the early train, she wouldn't arrive until 8:20, which was unacceptable to my client.

One week, the client had a big project that needed to be finished within a tight deadline. The office assistant stayed late three days in a row to help complete the project and was exhausted. On Friday of that week, she overslept, missed the early bus, and showed up to work at 8:20 A.M. My client took that as yet another example of someone taking advantage of her, not showing up on time. She mentioned to the office assistant, in a nice but firm tone, that she would appreciate if that never happened again.

At first, the office assistant was crushed and humiliated. Then she got mad. From that day forward, she started to show up at the office at 7:30, and drink coffee and read the paper until exactly 8:00 A.M. She would leave at the stroke of 5:00 P.M. She took every minute of her hour for lunch, even if there was a pressing project. She stopped caring and didn't work as hard. My client bemoaned the fact that here was yet another person who didn't want to work for the money she was paid, who didn't care and was taking advantage of her. It was amazing.

The paranoia of the leader was also emulated by many of her top managers, who were also quick to question and accuse. It was a difficult environment, with extremely high turnover at all levels.

The Micromanager

The most common issue I see is the classic micromanager. I can't tell you how many times I've witnessed the entrepreneur/leader play this game. The entrepreneur has had every job from the ground up from the very beginning. No one else can drum up business, make a sales call, service an account, fill out a contract, even answer the phone like the entrepreneur! Now that business is humming, many employees are in place to handle small tasks and big responsibilities. And yet the entrepreneur often has trouble letting go. Decision after decision, from handling a difficult client to buying stamps, has to receive the express blessing of the leader. Employees are not empowered, and the entrepreneur is stressed and stretched to the max—but feels indispensable. That's the key to this scenario. This is the point at which growth stops or is slowed for many businesses—the point at which the entrepreneur can't let go. This can create an environment of frustration and high turnover.

The Jellyfish

Let's take one more easy example—the people who can't say no or set boundaries. No matter how busy they are or how unappealing the new project seems, they will jump at business. This obviously trickles down to their people. Pretty soon everyone is swamped, tired, grumpy and a little resentful. But the bottom line is, it's set up so it's not OK to say no. This is a problem I've had myself. The first step is to admit you have a problem!

I watched as one client, whose company differentiated itself through quality of its services and its personalized approach, took on a huge project on sheer guts, figuring she'd find the people and set up the processes to take it on. She did, but it took a while and quality slipped to the extent that she lost the client's trust. When the contract came up for renewal, she lost it without even being asked to submit a proposal.

Acknowledging Your Issues Is the First Step

IF YOU ARE willing to recognize your own issues and understand how your behaviors are creating a negative situation in your company, you can probably fix or at least improve the problems. Of course, you must be willing to work on the issues head-on, and you must be willing to listen to and trust those around you, including your employees, to work with you to change the behaviors. It may take a while—especially because people tend to revert back to behaviors in times of stress. It may also require training, but it can be done. However, if you are unwilling to recognize negative behavior patterns in your company or own up to your role in it, the problems will continue to fester.

What issues or challenges do you have?

What negative patterns do you play out over and over?

In what areas are you lacking?

How could these issues manifest themselves in your company?

What can you do to keep these issues from being played out in your company?

Your Company

Authentic Marketing

HOW DOES BEING honest with your business, both in terms of how you run it and how you communicate it to others, attract clients?

It all has to do with branding and identity. Let's define these terms, because every aspiring entrepreneur needs to understand what they are and how they're created. Very simply put, a brand is another person's perception of your product or service. Identity is their view of your company. And that is what marketing is all about.

A strong, successful brand is one that is clear, basic, and accepted by lots of people. It's a simple characteristic or identity that everyone associates with your product or service. The obvious example everyone always uses is Volvo. Volvo means safety. You can ask almost everyone you know what Volvo stands for, and they will all give that answer. Another obvious example you hear all the time is the Ritz-Carlton. The Ritz is synonymous with quality. Those are good, clear brands.

But how do you effectively create a brand? How do you decide what it should be, in the first place?

A traditional perspective on marketing is to talk to prospective customers to determine their needs, find out what they think they want, and then figure out a way to fill that need. Conventional marketing wisdom is that market research—especially client input—should drive the creation of a business. People want flashy? Then give them flashy. But I think of it this way. It's like a person saying, "I'd like to have a relationship with you. Who do you want me to be? How would you like me to act?"

It's hard to try to be something you're not just to please somebody else. The spark that makes you who you are can never survive, and then you are less attractive to them anyway. This is what happens to many new companies who listen too closely to potential clients.

Here's how I differ from those who hold the traditional view of branding: I believe that truth exists from within the essence of the company, and that people are extremely good at perceiving truth and artifice, especially when it comes to marketing. We are incredibly intuitive, not to mention pretty savvy consumers. Even if we get it wrong initially, over time, we usually are able to figure it out. Instead of trying to create or build a brand in a traditional sense, the idea is to know yourself and then be yourself. Marketing then becomes honestly expressing who you are.

The truth of a company, like a person, comes from the inside.

I'm not suggesting that you ignore potential customers while creating your business. On the contrary. I think it is great to involve them early on as you go through the birthing process, as well as to gather information when you need it. Understanding who they are and what they want is crucial. But when the rubber hits the road, you need to be true to yourself and your company.

When Jim started his company writing music for commercials, he faced a crowded field of competitors, all vying for business from writers, producers, and creative directors at ad agencies. His competitors had trendy marketing programs built on shock value, all designed to get the attention of cool, blasé creatives.

Initially, Jim wanted to come up with an approach similar to those of his competitors. But nothing seemed to fit. They simply did not express who he was. An earnest musician and devoted Buddhist, he was anything but trendy in the vein of the other music houses. We decided to take a more honest approach to what he and his company are about. We named his company Earthborne Music and developed an identity with an earthy, connected feel that represented the best of who he was and what he wanted his company to be. This identity also happened to differentiate him from everyone else, which meant his ads really stood out, and, along with his direct mail and web site, got a great deal of attention and positive feedback from a group of potential clients who are normally hard to impress.

"When I write music, I create pieces that I love, that really have something happening," says Jim. "I know that if I just try to give clients what I think they want, it never works as well. I don't feel as good about it, and ultimately they don't either. I realized the same thing was true for developing my company's identity and marketing plan. Even if it wasn't what everyone else was doing, I had to be real."

What qualities, or brand attributes, describe your company?

What three to five adjectives would you want a customer to use after working with your company, or buying your products, or utilizing your service?

What type of experience would you want your customers to have? Describe the entire experience in depth.

What major skills and talents, or core competencies, will your company have?

What issues and challenges (market or otherwise) will your company face in becoming the type of company you want it to be?

How to Capture Your Company's Personality

CAPTURING YOUR COMPANY'S personality is an essential part of developing your identity. It impacts your communications, your interactions, and your human resource efforts, for one thing.

Whenever I begin to work with a new company, one of the first things I do is attempt to understand its culture and personality. Because personality can be difficult to define, and because it is a creative and organic, as opposed to dry and static, thing, I have created some fun exercises to help people describe what the company is like. I often have a client or a group of employees answer a bunch of lighthearted questions, without giving them too much thought. I like to do this with a group because it's more fun and takes the heaviness out of the process. Often, people's reasoning provokes laughter and lighthearted discussion.

Is your company best described as . . .

- ocean or mountains?
- Beatles or Stones?
- Jazz or reggae?
- Toyota or Mercedes?
- flower or plant?
- winter or summer?
- spring or fall?
- theater or film?
- comedy or drama?
- chicken or steak?
- fruit or vegetable?
- cottage or condo?
- sonnet or byte?
- rural or urban?
- Coke or 7Up?
- sugar or spice?

- sun or ski?
- cat or dog?
- symphony or rock concert?
- train or plane?
- Han Solo or Luke Skywalker?
- Audrey Hepburn or Marilyn Monroe?
- hike or bike?
- coffee or tea?
- muted colors or primary colors?
- James Dean or Cary Grant?
- Leno or Letterman?

When clients are particularly creative and/or open to this kind of exercise, I often take it to the next level and ask them the Barbara Walters version of the same questions. I ask everyone in the group either to answer individually and then discuss their answers, or to decide the answer as a group. This is a fun and enlightening way to learn about the company (as well as the way the group interacts).

In reference to your company:

- If you were a car, what would you be and why?
- If you were a drink, what would you be and why?
- If you were a city, what would you be and why?
- If you were an animal, what would you be and why?
- If you were a musical genre, what would you be and why?
- If you were a type of food, who would you be and why?
- If you were a movie star, who would you be and why?
- If you were a color, what would you be and why?
- If you were a country, what would you be and why?
- If you were a talk show host, who would you be and why?
- If you were an artist, who would you be and why?
- If you were a historical era, what would you be and why?
- If you were a flower, what would you be and why?
- If you were a Spice Girl, who would you be and why?

Obviously, almost any question will do, as a starting point for shining the light on who you are. This is the type of information that anyone working with your company—from a designer to a PR person to a sales or marketing person—will be grateful to have in trying to communicate who you are. It also can give you a greater awareness of who you are—and who your employees think you are! (That can be a wake-up call for some leaders.)

This is also a great exercise to do when working with a group of employees, to learn about who they are by asking them to answer the questions for themselves as individuals, and then to answer the questions in reference to the company.

Two

Pursuing Joy

2. follow your passions

Many of the people I work with who are in the process of starting their own businesses are not typical entrepreneurs. They didn't begin with the thought: "I'd like to start a business." Instead, they held a deeply felt passion for something that that led them to start their own company.

Passion is enthusiasm, interest, love. People pick up on and are attracted to that positive energy, that buzz of excitement. It's just like when you are having a really great day, and you're happy and excited about life—people just want to be around you. It's true for companies, too. Passion is the magic that makes a company's products and services stand out from the crowd.

Companies often try to create that excitement through advertising. There are some great ads and commercials that do have that passionate buzz, but often in our media-savvy culture, people just really like the advertising—not the product.

Besides, advertising is expensive and often is not the most effective use of your money when you first start out.

One of the keys to having a happy and successful life is to build it around your passions. That is also a key to having a successful company. If you're doing what you love, you will have more energy and more desire to make it work and get through the hard times. If you care about your company, odds are you'll go the extra mile to make it more special.

Visiting the Food Angel

THE FOOD ANGEL, as my friends and I named him, was the cook at a tiny Middle Eastern restaurant in the heart of Old Town in Chicago. We went to this restaurant often, and inevitably, within minutes, the tiny, round cook would see us and run out of the kitchen past the waiters, yelling, "Hellooooooo!" We would order from him what we always did, and he would ignore us and say, "I make something special for you! I want you hap-pee!"

He'd run back into the kitchen, where we could see him running this way and that, chopping, mixing, and sautéing. Then he would bring out dish after dish of absolutely amazing food and beam at us as we happily dug in. His passion was making people happy through his cooking.

After a while, the Food Angel disappeared, and a new cook took his place. The food tasted sort of the same, but it just wasn't as good. We stopped going.

It was missing the magic ingredient. Passion.

Mining Your Passions

MANY ENTREPRENEURS HAVE profound passion for their product or service. For example, in *Harvests of Joy,* pioneering California winemaker Robert Mondavi's memoir of his life growing grapes and making wine, he writes, "Wine to me is a passion. It's family and friends. It's warmth of heart and generosity of spirit. Wine is art. It's culture. It's the essence of civilization and the Art of Living. Wine had been with us for seven thousand years, almost since the dawn of civilization, and for centuries poets, painters, musicians, and philosophers have sung its praises. Even the Bible applauds its virtues. And wine to me is even more. When I pour a glass of truly fine wine, when I hold it up to the light and admire its color, when I raise it to my nose and savor its bouquet and essence, I know that wine is, above all else, a blessing, a gift of nature, a joy as pure and elemental as the soil and vines and sunshine from which it springs. 'Wine is life,' Petronius said two thousand years ago, and I know exactly what he meant."

Who wouldn't want to buy wine from this guy?

Other entrepreneurs have a passion for the challenge of running their business; they don't really care what the business is. I have one client—or potential client, I should say—who desperately wants to start her own business, but she still has no idea what it will be. She just wants to build a company up from scratch according to her vision. She loves managing people, serving customers, and handling money . . . and pretty much everything about running a business.

In the end, it doesn't matter which aspect of starting your company is most important to you, as long as you have a passion that will sustain you.

What are your one or two greatest passions in life?

What do they mean to you? What do they represent? How do they make you feel?

Write a statement for each of your greatest passions, about what each means for you, in the spirit of Robert Mondavi's above.

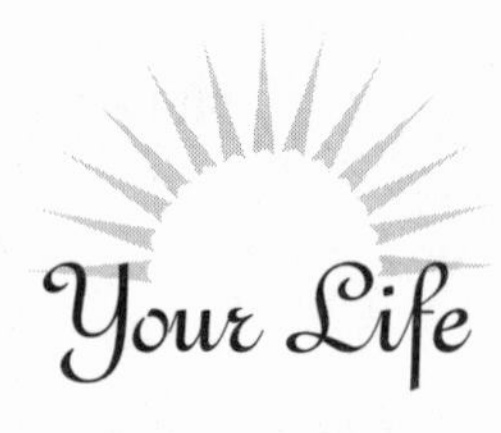

Your Life

You Sell What?

AS A FRESHMAN in college, I spent a few days in a vineyard town in California with a friend. The first time we drove through the main square of the small downtown, we spotted a curious little store. It was so curious, in fact, that we drove past it three times to get a closer look.

The store contained white ceramic ducks with blue bows around their necks. That may not seem strange in itself, until you realize that white ceramic ducks with blue bows was all it sold. Ducks sitting looking straight ahead. Ducks sitting looking right or left. Ducks sitting with outstretched necks. Rows and rows of white ceramic ducks with blue bows, from floor to ceiling.

We were amazed and, frankly, a little unnerved.

"Can you say drug front?" said my friend.

I didn't know what to make of it then, but now I choose to think that somebody in that small California town just absolutely loved white ceramic ducks. And beyond that, I believe that if a person's passion for white ceramic ducks could lead him or her to open a whole store, then somewhere out there, a whole lot more people must be clamoring to buy those ducks.

Stranger things have happened. Like Pet Rocks. Like Beanie Babies.

Maybe that store is still right there on the main square of that town, fourteen years later. Maybe it has expanded. Maybe someday there will be one on my corner.

You never know. The important thing is not to judge anyone's dreams and passions, including your own.

Anything Is Sacred If It Comes from Your Heart.

ONE OF THE keys to living from your heart is doing what you absolutely love to do. That love is the most solid foundation for any company. Secretly, or maybe not so secretly, we all want the fruits of our labor to be meaningful and valuable. But how do you know what your life's work is?

The first clue is what we loved as children.

As a young child, chances are good that your passions and dreams were still pure. It's all about what you want to do, not about what you want to achieve or what that says about who you think you are.

When I was five years old, I wanted to write. Publishing, producing, critical approval, and payment never entered the equation. My love for writing and storytelling is at the heart of both my marketing consulting work and my creative pursuits.

Happily, if spiritual masters great and small are to be believed, when you do what you love, abundance—and more importantly, meaning and fulfillment—will follow. The key is getting back to what you love.

What were your dreams as a child? Do you still harbor any of those dreams secretly?

What are the things you love, or love to do? What are the things that make life worth living for you? This can include anything from acting to your dog to Ben & Jerry's chocolate chip cookie dough ice cream. List all of the hobbies, causes, and other things you passionately care about.

For each passion, think about how much time you spend pursuing it. Which of your passions really play a major part in your life?

What is keeping you from pursuing the passions you do not allow yourself?

What can you do to get a little more of those passions into your life?

Choose one passion you are missing in your life, and commit to yourself that you will make time for it this week, even if it's just for ten minutes.

Your Company

Building Your Company on Your Passions

I CAN TELL almost immediately when I meet with a new client whether or not they have passion for their idea or company. You can feel it as soon as you walk in the door. There's an energy, an aliveness, in the air, even when times are tough or people are working extremely hard. People who have passion for their idea generate an indefinable energy that often radiates throughout the company. It's exciting to work with people like that and to watch as their ideas take form and as others are caught up in the excitement.

On the other hand, it's rare to meet an excited, enthusiastic employee of companies run by people who have lost—or never had—passion for their idea. It usually feels like people are just putting in time (sometimes a lot of time). A heaviness, or at the very least a sense of apathy, seems to hang in the air.

If your idea for a company does not give you energy, it's important to look at that and ask yourself some tough questions.

- Why is your idea draining you instead of energizing you?
- Why have you chosen this idea?
- Are you passionate enough about this idea to sustain you through the hard times?
- If you decide this is the wrong idea, is there another idea that you really want to pursue, but don't think you have the time, ability, experience, or resources? Are you willing to expand or change your vision to include that idea or company as a possibility? If not, what is standing in your way?

If you are feeling drained by your idea because you are worried or afraid, and not because of a lack of passion, take heart—it may not be as hard as you think to make it work, if you let your passion guide you.

One example is a client of mine, Kevin, an actor, whose passion for a certain play and certain types of roles led him to begin a theater company. He never expected to start his own company, but his passions led him there. He says, "One day as I was ranting about my frustrations as an actor, my friend Eric asked me, 'Well, what types of parts would you like to do?' I had been carrying a play around for a few months. In it, a man and woman running from their pasts are thrown together and forced to confront themselves. I felt a strong connection to both the play's message of healing and to the part. So I answered Eric by telling him this is a production I'd love to do. Eric responded with 'Well, I've got some money.'

"It hit like a thunderclap, that it was possible to put up my own show. From that seed sprung more and more questions. We would meet on Sundays, and Eric would push me to look toward the future, when mostly all I wanted was to do the play. But through his prodding and my secret dream of working with a committed group of actors, I learned to expand my vision into a theater company."

Kevin's vision of his theater company continues to expand, also including outreach and classes.

Starbucks is a great example of a company that was created from several of its founders' and leaders' passions, as current CEO Howard Schultz describes in *Pour Your Heart into It.* The original founders were not businesspeople. They were three very different men who shared an abiding love of high-quality coffee. Schultz himself originally fell in love with the business because of the passion of its founders, which he encountered at his first meeting with founder Jerry Baldwin. He writes, "Although Jerry didn't discuss marketing plans or sales strategies, I was beginning to see he had a business philosophy the likes of which I had never encountered. First, every company must stand for something. Starbucks stood not only for good coffee, but specifically for the dark-roasted flavor that the founders were passionate about. That's what differentiated it and made it authentic."

In turn, Schultz's passion for the community and romance of the cafés in Italy, as well as his desire to lead a company that took care of its people, drove Starbucks' second phase of growth. It kept him energized through the many challenges he faced transforming the company.

Which of your passions does your idea and company directly address?

Write at least a page on how your idea or your company captures one or more of your passions.

Make Room for Your Other Passions, Too.

OF COURSE, YOU probably have lots of passions, more than can be encompassed directly by your company.

If your business does not incorporate certain of your passions, you can always find ways to deal with them indirectly. For example, one client, who runs a web site development company, loves windsurfing and sailing. He has networked extensively in the windsurfing community, marketing within certain groups and associations. He also sails competitively, and has his logo painted on the side of one of the boats. He has joined one of the local yacht clubs as a place to hold meetings and take his clients to lunch. His own web site includes a nautical theme.

Which of your passions could your company indirectly address? How?

How to Create a Space That Supports Your Passion

ONE WAY TO help ensure that your work comes from a place of heart and passion is to make your office or work space a beautiful, inspiring place that reflects the things and people you care about and helps keep your heart open as you work. You can do this with pictures of people you love, music that inspires you, candles, colors, photographs (not necessarily of people), artwork, plants, books, lamps, and quotes or symbols that remind you why you're doing this.

1. REALIZE WHAT YOUR SPACE CAN TEACH YOU.

   Here's a great little exercise that almost always has an interesting outcome. Take a look at the space from which you are creating or running your company. Observe without judgment. What is in your space? What is clean? What is cluttered? What gets prime focus? What is shoved in piles or in the corner? What colors do you see in your space? What feeling do you get when you look at it objectively? What aspects of your space do you love? What aspects of your space are you not so crazy about? If you were a stranger, what would this space tell you about the person who uses it? Does this space appear productive? Happy? Creative? As a stranger, what would you think the person who uses this space values?

2. IMAGINE YOUR IDEAL SPACE.

   Now imagine your ultimate ideal space from which to create or manage your company, if money were no object. This is especially helpful if you can do it from a meditative space, quieting your mind, perhaps focusing on a flame or your breath, listening to a tape of chants, or repeating a mantra. When you've cleared your mind, ask yourself what your ideal creative space would be like. Sky's the limit—urban loft, beachside cottage, a beautifully done extra bedroom, a large office building made of glass—let the image come to you. Let yourself see the furniture, the paint on the walls, the colors, the lights, the flooring, the decorations. What feeling do you get from your ideal space? What colors and textures do you see? Jot down what you see in a notebook. Then ask yourself what elements of that ideal space you can incorporate into your current space. It may be a painted wall or a less cluttered feel or even a symbol that reminds you of your ultimate space. Write down several things you can do with your current space to approximate this ideal space you see in your mind's eye.

3. CLEAR YOUR SPACE.

   Clear your current space of clutter or of any unwanted elements that you can live without to make way for the things that keep your heart open and your creativity flowing. Get rid of anything in your space that does not serve your work directly or indirectly. Try to recreate the feeling of the ultimate space you imagined, even if it's just in a symbolic way. Be creative!

4. PREPARE YOUR SPACE.

- First you need to get organized. Think through your work processes and priorities, and design your space to serve your major functions effectively. Keep the things you need often close by, where you can easily access them, and find a system that works for you in terms of storing and filing. If you have a problem with clutter, you may need to find some inexpensive organization tools such as shelving—but think it through first before you buy anything. Throw away everything you don't need as you get it—it adds up! If you have trouble doing this on your own, ask an organized friend to work through it with you, or find a consultant who specializes in this kind of thing or a book that can guide you (there are several on the market).
- Add your new elements. A new coat of paint, photos, chimes, whatever. . . . Now is the time to add anything you need to keep your passions and heart front and center. Homemade touches are nice—a painted tile, a drawing, or a note from someone you love can help keep you in a positive frame of mind.

5. INITIATE YOUR SPACE.

   Make a commitment, say a prayer, create a ritual to honor the sacredness of the space and the work you will be doing there. Add at least one element that exists purely to remind you of the sacred nature of your work.

6. BE FLEXIBLE AND CREATIVE AS YOUR WORK EVOLVES.

   Be aware of what you like or don't like about your newly designed space. If anything isn't working for you, change it. Try out different ways to organize your space. Move things around. Add some chimes or a new picture and see how it works for you. The key is to have a space that supports your creativity and opens your heart.

Climbing the Right Mountain

3. define success for yourself

YOUR COMPANY IS only part of your life. And that's all it should be. But time and again, I see entrepreneurs, small business owners, corporate managers, and executives working themselves to the bone, out of balance and unfulfilled in other areas of their life. Hey, I've been there. It's hard not to get caught up in that.

That's why it's wise to start with a holistic view of your life. Even if you know exactly what you want to do, and you can envision your company, it can't hurt to take a few minutes and really think about your life in the larger perspective. It could help you protect your peace of mind in the long run, and it will help you ensure from the beginning that you are working toward the things that really matter to you.

Get Down to What Really Matters

SOMETIMES WE FORGET what's really important because we get caught up in the numbers.

I recently had an amazingly vivid dream in which an ex-boyfriend (of the rare true-love variety) showed up unexpectedly at my door. The last time I had seen him, I was twenty-four years old and a size four—and there I was, very conscious that I was ten years older, looking my worst in sweats with messy hair and no makeup.

Interestingly, in the dream, he looked about twenty years older than he is, was puffy and balding, and had on an exceedingly bad suit. He said he had given up on his medical career because he really just wanted to sell timeshares. He was using really bad grammar, and did I mention the suit?

But it was *him*, and I felt all the love for him I always had, completely unaffected by his new look or career choices. I knew that, given the chance, I would follow him anywhere. Shack up in a mobile home and eat cheese from a can? I was all over it. I could write brochures about timeshares!

I woke up and thought how feeling that love for someone made me realize how superficial and judgmental my thoughts and beliefs were, mainly about myself. Was it time to forever let go of the numbers twenty-four and four? Do I really need to be Britney Spears to experience love?

I started to think about what is behind the numbers, and the things, that we are so desperate to obtain. What do they symbolize?

Do I really need a million dollars, or do I just want a nice life with freedom to create? (And don't I have that already?) Do I really need a specific award, or do I actually want to do work that touches and inspires people? And if I don't believe I matter now, how can a certain sum of money and a house on Nantucket really help? Not that it's wrong to want those things, but it's certainly counterproductive to believe I need them to be whole.

So many people get everything they think they want, and then they realize that none of those things make them happy. Why not focus on what I have already, and what I want more of, and what I want to do and create for others? One of the beautiful paradoxes of the universe (though I can't prove this) is that when you let go of the numbers and the symbols and focus instead on what's real, you may reach or surpass those numbers anyway. But it won't matter that much anyway, because you'll already be happy.

Staying in Balance

STARTING FROM THE perspective of what really matters will help keep us in balance, but it's just a start. As an entrepreneur, the temptations to lose sight of balance are immense. It's important to keep an eye on this issue, from the very beginning (but it's never too late to change).

Odds are you've heard all the stories about what it takes to be a successful entrepreneur. All you do is work. You never sleep. You never see your kids or your friends. You can kiss those hobbies good-bye.

This conventional wisdom is reinforced by the experts. Joseph Boyett and Jimmie Boyett studied the lives and careers of many successful entrepreneurs and concluded in their book, *The Guru Guide to Entrepreneurship,* that one of the requirements to succeeding as an entrepreneur is to "sacrifice your personal life." They say that the successful entrepreneurs they studied "describe their lives as consisting mostly of work, particularly during the early years of starting their businesses."

Boyett and Boyett say the entrepreneurs worked so hard "because they had to."

I respectfully disagree. They didn't have to. Bill Gates chose to build Microsoft to the scope it is. They all chose to grow their companies as quickly and as large as they did. But not all entrepreneurs are driven to grow so fast or so large.

Besides, this drive to work constantly, to be as big as possible, is not solely the domain of entrepreneurs. This is the same urge that makes corporate executives, students, nurses—people of all professions, in fact—work their fingers to the bone. It is an American phenomenon. I have battled the disease of workaholism myself.

Why do we do it, really? I see entrepreneurs and leaders all the time who complain about how they never have a minute to themselves, and then don't let the people who work for them make a single decision on their own. Or they go after the next big deal without having enough people to get the job done. They build their own prisons.

This need to work all the time, to sacrifice, to grow at all costs, is problematic. It's a myth. It's another way to convince ourselves or others that we are trapped, that we can't control our destinies. You want to start your own company? OK then, prevailing wisdom says, you're going to have to sacrifice your whole life. Well, I don't buy it.

It's all about deciding what you need to be happy. How much money do you need? How much stuff? How much time?

In my corporate life, I was rich in funds, but poverty-stricken in terms of time. When I left and started my own company, I had a specific goal: to make enough money working twenty hours a week to support myself so that I could spend the rest of the time on my creative projects. I had to change my lifestyle. I had to decide I didn't need to own a house yet. I had to let go of my need to be viewed as a success in traditional terms. I had to constantly battle the temptation to do more and more work, leaving less time for my creativity. I had to turn down lucrative, prestigious full-time jobs when I was worried about late invoices that I needed to pay my rent. And, at this point, I'm a lot poorer than I would have been had I stuck around to cash in all those stock options, but I sure am happy. In my eyes, my humble company is a rousing success. And I believe, if I follow my heart and true passions, I will continue to experience greater abundance.

Sometimes Things Are Easy

EVEN IF YOU do want your company to be a huge enterprise or make tons of money, do you really have to work so hard that you'll have no life? The whole idea of having to work ourselves to the bone to create success is a powerful shared belief, as well as an effective way to torture ourselves, harm our health and hide from real life. (Or it's something we can complain about while we're secretly enjoying ourselves!) Don't get me wrong, I believe that hard work pays off—but I think it doesn't always have to be so hard. The universe can be quite helpful.

Sometimes things are easy . . . especially when you're following your path.

One client of mine left his job as a software engineer and started his own consulting firm with the hope of having a more balanced life. Without ever marketing himself, he has supported himself well, making a high hourly rate on jobs that have basically fallen in his lap. With his rate, he can match his old salary working less than half the time, which leaves him plenty of space in his life for traveling, taking classes, and enjoying his life.

Another client left her job as a copywriter at an ad agency to strike out on her own and spend more time with her family and on her own creative writing. She also can make or surpass her previous job's salary by working less than twenty hours a week, given her hourly rate. She's also found it relatively simple to find work without having to market herself.

Go figure.

My first real experience with this type of surprising ease was at one of my first jobs as an employee communications person for a large company, when I helped start a community service team. My roommate, Katie, was a French teacher at a school for gifted children on the South Side of Chicago. The stories she told about the school's lack of resources for these incredible children—not enough paper, no art supplies—bothered me.

I asked one of the executives if we could start a team to do community service, and she gave me permission and resources on the spot. I booked a conference room and sent out a company-wide memo. Two days later, nearly forty people crowded into a small conference room. In an hour, we had developed our mission and brainstormed some projects. I told the group about my roommate's school and suggested starting a partnership program. The team voted to take on the project, along with a number of other projects.

The next week, we held a three-day school supply drive. The response was overwhelming. I stopped by the lobby every couple hours as box after box filled up with paper, notebooks, glue, scissors, markers, crayons, rulers. . . . We collected hundreds of pounds of school and art supplies, along with thousands of dollars (including an anonymous five-hundred-dollar donation). The company contributed boxes of outdated letterhead and twelve older computers.

The faculty at the school was overwhelmed. The kids used the art supplies to write and draw thank-you notes, which we displayed. The employees were even more touched than the children were.

The partnership program grew from there. Our people visited often, running career days and judging art and science fairs. We sponsored visits by improv troupes and literary contests. The children visited us at our offices, delighting in what would be for many their first-ever elevator ride, and drinking in the views of the city from the twenty-seventh floor. They wrote stories and poems that were published in our newsletters. Their drawings became our company holiday cards. The relationship lived on long after my roommate left the school and I left the company.

The amazing thing was, it was so easy. Truly, it was almost effortless, and unbelievably fulfilling. It was bigger than any of us. A need met a desire to help, or maybe another need, and the results were astonishing. I couldn't take any real responsibility for its success; in fact, I couldn't have stopped it from happening if I tried.

Lisa Holmes describes a similar experience with her nonprofit, Whimsy City, which seemed to magnetically attract support:

"As I mentioned the idea for Whimsy City, just vaguely, in passing, I found people absolutely flocked to it. Whimsy City was like a magnet, drawing people and resources in faster than I could think. I hardly had to utter the words and people would be saying, 'I'll help. What can I do?' They offered up research materials, provided free rehearsal space, offered to be on the board, or to help with fund-raising. My sister came up with the name. A neighbor lugged over some books on grant writing.

"This thing, that I didn't even want to start, really . . . was ending up to be the easiest thing I've ever tried to do. . . . I'm resolved to letting it flow . . . letting it become what it's meant to become. It doesn't seem like I can stop it anyway."

IN *THE CORPORATE MYSTIC*, consultants Gay Hendricks and Kate Ludeman explore the secrets of "corporate mystics," or leaders "who seem to operate on a level of effectiveness that appears esoteric" and who "are in business for their hearts and souls as well as their wallets." They say, "To get more done by doing less is a credo and a key operating style of corporate mystics. They put a great deal of attention on learning to be in the present because they have found that this is the only place from which time can be expanded. If you are in the present—not caught up in regret about

the past or anxiety about the future—time essentially becomes malleable. When you are in the grip of the past or the future, there is never enough time, because you are trying to be in two places at once. If you are standing in the present while your mind is somewhere else, there is a fundamental split that produces pressure and tension. . . . When time pressures begin to creep in, they use this as feedback that they are not centering themselves in the present."

Your Life

I'VE NOTICED THAT often people get so caught up in driving the success of their company that they start to personally suffer. They have definitions of success for their companies that seem to clash with their definitions of success in their own personal lives. My philosophy with my clients is to start with what you want out of life first. Otherwise, we get it all backward. And again, the important thing is to keep digging deeper underneath the things you want. For example, if you say, "I want to retire by the age of forty," ask yourself why? If your answer is, "I want free time," ask why? If you answer, "I want to travel and spend time with my family," ask why not make some time to do that now? Clearly think through what you want, and consider if there's an even better way to experience it.

Define Success for Yourself

What does success mean to you?

What are you most proud of in your life?

What do you hope people will say about you when you die?

Imagine that you are at a future point in your life, living it successfully according to your definition. Write a letter to yourself about how that feels and include encouraging words to yourself about how to get there. (We always give ourselves the best advice, have you noticed? Although we may not always stop to listen. . . .)

Write a promise to yourself that you will live a successful life, date it, and sign your full name.

Write an affirmation to yourself and say it to yourself as often as you can for a week. For example, if your definition of success is "learning and growing," your affirmation can be "I am learning and growing every day."

If it helps you, find an object or symbol that will remind you of what success means to you in the larger sense. Keep it in a safe place where you can look at it often.

Identify Your Needs

OK, CARDS ON the table. What do you need to fully enjoy life? Bottom line, what can you not live without, financially, emotionally, spiritually? I need to write and work out. I need books, music, laughter, conversation, artistic collaboration. I need my cats, sunshine, the ocean, freedom, fun, challenge, a quiet place to write, travel, time for myself, time with family and friends, soy chai lattès, U2 tickets. All crucial!

It's important to know your basic needs, so you can design your company and your life to meet them. It's especially important to know the first couple years of a new business, when you may need to scale your lifestyle back a little.

What are the things you need to be happy, bottom line? This could include things like time alone, time with family, meaningful work, a healthy lifestyle, etc.

Explore Your Desires

HERE'S WHERE YOU get to dream big. Do you want to retire at fifty? Do you want to live in the mountains or by the ocean? These are important things to know as you envision your company and your life.

Be shamelessly superficial! Be open to abundance! I want a nice computer, a green VW bug, a house on Nantucket big enough for family and friends, and an Oscar! Isn't it hard? Don't you feel guilty? Do it anyway! I won't tell.

What are the things you want out of life? They can be big or small, short-term or long-term, and can include anything from a new car to a family to career success.

Write a page on what a balanced life looks like for you. How will you balance your work with family, friends, and your physical, emotional, mental, and spiritual well-being? How will you have fun?

Your Company

Define Success for Your Company

THE DANGER, ONCE again, is to get caught up in the numbers. And the solution is to make sure you understand what's behind the numbers. Also, you need to make sure your short-term goals lead you to your long-term goals.

I often find that clients set arbitrary short-term goals that do not seem to lead them to what they say their long-term goals are. For example, they want to open an office in two more cities by the end of the year, or grow their revenues to $10 million, or add three product lines by March. Yet their long-term goal is to be the number-one company in the city in terms of quality, or to attract a buyer so they can retire . . . and their short-term goals leave them no time or energy to pursue their long-term goal, and seem to dilute their ability to achieve it. Growth at all costs may be expensive, or it may dilute your differentiating qualities, or it may distract you from your goal of having a successful business that allows you to spend more time with your family.

It's important to know, and then to remember, what your ultimate definition of success is for your company, especially in terms of how it fits in with your goals for your life.

How do you define success for your company?

How much money do you want your company to make, and how much of that do you want to take home in salary?

What significant goals would you like your company to reach in the next year? The next two years? The next five years?

Why do you want to achieve these goals? What are the underlying values behind your desire to achieve? Is this your highest perspective? Does this definition of success for your company help you achieve your personal definition of success?

Will these goals meet your needs and desires, as well as your need for balance? If not, how else can you achieve what you want and need? Is there anything you're willing to compromise in the short-term?

Write your ultimate definition of success for your company. And then put it in a place where you can see it every day!

Let Your Imagination Run Wild

IMAGINING WHAT IS possible is an important step in doing your part to help create it. Just as star athletes visualize performing at peak capacity to help improve their own performance, you can pave the way for your future success by letting yourself experience your desires. This is the part where you get to fantasize!

What would you like for your company?

In your wildest imaginings, what would your company be like? Would you be bigger than Bill Gates? Would you have a beautiful office filled with happy employees? Would you be inventing products that help people live better lives? What is your ultimate fantasy?

What would you like from your company for yourself? Let yourself dream big!

How to Communicate and Measure Success

1. *Consider and reflect on what your ultimate definition of success is for your company.*

   The most important thing is to know what you want your company to achieve and to be able to explain it in basic, human, simple terms. Of course, you may have some goals you don't want to share with everyone—for example, selling the company or merging with another company—for legal or personal reasons. But share what you can, because your employees will feel empowered and respected, and chances are greater that they will get behind your goals and work together to try to achieve them.

2. *Define simple, practical ways to achieve that definition of success.*

   It's important to explain to your people how they can play a role in achieving your ultimate goals. For example, if one of your ultimate definitions of success is to help physically challenged people with your technology, then explain how you will achieve that: say, by developing specific applications of your products and services that improve their quality of living.

   Another easier example is financial. If your goal is to become a $10 million company by the year 2005, outline your basic financial goals so your employees will see how you can get there.

3. *Measure how well you are achieving your definition of success.*

   Once you have outlined the ways you can achieve success, then you need to keep track of how you are doing. Using the previous example, you can document the new products and services you have created. You can also keep track of how well they are selling, and do simple customer research to determine if the clients are happy with the results. You should keep the measurements simple, and commit to consistently capturing your progress.

4. *Acknowledge what you are doing well and what you need to improve upon.*

   It takes courage to measure things, because you may find that you're not doing as well as you expected in some areas. But, of course, it's important to know.

   I've noticed an interesting phenomenon when people are presented with bad results that they do not expect. First, they question the messenger (as well they should). Who are these people that did this research? What are their qualifications? Who are their other clients? Then they question the numbers (also smart). How did you come up with these numbers anyway? What assumptions did you make? Did you consider this or that? Then, sometimes, they blame the employees or each other (let's not go there). Fifth, they listen, they let it sink in, and they decide what to do. It's OK; it's messy and human. And as long as they reach the point where they can hear the truth, then they've really gotten somewhere.

   If you're ever in this position, look honestly at your measurements and own up to what is working or not. It's tempting to close your eyes or to make excuses when the results you'd like are just not there—but sticking your head in the sand is never the answer (but often the response). Do a little soul-searching, brain-storming, self-analysis or company-analysis.

5. *Communicate your status.*

   Feed back the results of your measurements to your people, along with an explanation of why the results are what they are, and how to improve things. Add your encouragement, thanks, inspiration, explanations, thoughts, or challenges. The act of keeping your people informed tells them that they play an important part in the success of your company.

6. *Celebrate your achievements.*

   When your company is doing well, celebrate it! Do something fun as a group. This is a good way to show your gratitude and respect for your people. Beyond bonuses and rewards, why not throw an impromptu pizza party? Bagel Tuesdays? A trip to the nearest amusement park or outdoor summer concert? Celebrating together is a great way to build morale and team spirit.

7. *Solicit and reward positive and negative feedback.*

   Nobody knows better what is working or not and how to fix things than the people who are doing the work. An open-door policy is a great way to unearth ideas and information that may be helpful. Even if you don't use or agree with any of the ideas or feedback, be open, grateful and respectful. The first time an employee suffers negative consequences from sharing their thoughts is the end of open communication.

8. *Refine and continue.*

   If your goals shift, or if your measurements are not helpful enough, by all means change them—but explain why you are making changes. If you appear to drop your focus or stop measuring, it will hurt your credibility. You must remain committed and keep communicating.

IT'S AN INTERESTING exercise to compare your definition of success with where you are focusing your time and energy. There's often quite a gap. Here is a sample of answers I've gotten to the following questions:

What does success mean to you?

- *Success is just being comfortable walking around in your own skin . . . being content exactly where you are, and knowing that it's all happening perfectly.*
- *Feeling good about myself and giving the best of myself to those I love.*
- *Knowing what I want to do with my life (which is easily half the battle), and then having the courage to do it.*
- *Spending the majority of my time in a state of positive energy, making my art and cartoons and sharing my creations with as many people as possible.*

- *Making a positive personal impact on those close to me and developing good relationships with people I come into contact with.*
- *Raising a happy, healthy family. Making an honest living. Creating the best stories for business and for larger audiences that I can.*
- *Raising two fairly normal and happy children . . . and to have some effect, however small, on the improvement of the health of people.*
- *Happiness and contentment within.*
- *To have found full expression of my truest talents; to know joy in what you do (almost) every day and not defer joy.*
- *Making the most of each day in productive/useful activities flowing out of my basic core values—and presumably being true to them.*

What are you the most proud of in your life?

- *My ability to be honest with myself and the people who are important to me.*
- *My family, my recent work for clients, and the book I have under way.*
- *My time spent out of the U.S. experiencing other cultures and places and getting to know very different people. It gives you a dramatically changed perspective on what's important.*
- *The way I have been able to come to my own rescue during times of extreme personal and psychic crisis. I have done this by: learning to ask others for help; acknowledging and feeling unpleasant feelings (such as grief and anger) without fighting them; and retaining a sense of hope and trust in myself.*
- *Moving to Europe and all the personal and professional changes/challenges this entailed.*
- *That I helped others reach their goals.*
- *The friendships I have made and the people whose lives I have added something to . . . [and] the times I have been able to help someone out, even if just emotionally, and made them happier.*
- *Moments where I have given love unconditionally.*
- *My education and my kids.*
- *The times I followed a hunch, even just a micro voice, to do something "off the beaten track" and it panned out into something wonderful, with ripple effects.*

I'm proud of the times I worked on something with full resolve and heart and it showed in the product.

- *That by doing the above with due consideration for family and friends and colleagues, I seem to have done well enough to be placed in positions of influence with others. I'd be happy if I made other people's lives better one at a time and day by day and, if I'm lucky, by writing, teaching, or visible example.*

What do you want people to say about you when you die?

- *That I enjoyed myself, in every endeavor no matter how little or big.*
- *I was kind.*
- *Knowing me made a positive difference in someone's life.*
- *"She made the world a better place," or perhaps "I will really miss her."*
- *That my presence on the planet mattered.*
- *I was a good friend and always cared about others, and that I would drop what I was doing or give what I had to help.*
- *I was an honest guy you could count on. I made a difference in a lot of people's lives.*
- *That I knew what I wanted and really believed in myself. That I produced great work that will live on. That I was a good person.*
- *I was spirited. I knew low times but knew equally high times and didn't want to settle for safe.*

Four

Fulfilling Your Purpose

4. serve others by following your mission

Your mission is your individual reason for being on this planet. It is your unique way of serving yourself, others, and the world. It is what inspires you and fulfills you the most deeply. Similarly, your company's mission is its essential purpose.

We all long for meaning in our lives. Sure, other things drive us, too, but most of us are happiest when we feel like we are doing something that matters and is helpful to others. When your heartfelt goal is to serve others, you will have the weight of the universe behind you. You will find meaning, fulfillment, joy even. This will give you the strength to work through the difficult times.

Some people seem to be born knowing their mission. Others take longer to discover theirs. Sometimes it takes a disease, accident, or tragic loss to propel people into their mission. Michael J. Fox and Christopher Reeve have both transformed personal misfortune into world-changing missions to help people with, respectively, Parkinson's Disease and spinal cord injuries.

Sometimes your mission is connected to your personal struggles and lessons. One friend of mine dealt with debt for years, and ultimately became an inspired financial planner. Another friend, who had a long-standing battle with an extra few pounds, became a personal trainer. They've been in the trenches, they've fought the good fight and come out swinging! Another example is a client who had to hire home care to deal with illnesses in her family, and her experiences inspired her to start her own company providing the same type of care to others who found themselves in a similar situation to her own.

Harnessing the Business Power of Missions

STRONGLY AND HONESTLY building on an essential mission can benefit companies in many ways. First of all, the mission can keep a company focused as it grows. The company has an essential, baseline screen against which to weigh new products, services, or divisions. Simply put, does the change or addition help the company achieve its fundamental goals? Does it fall within the mission? If not, either the change is not useful or the mission needs to be adjusted.

Secondly, the mission may attract people who respect and value, perhaps even share, the same goals. The mission also can mobilize employees to work together for a higher purpose. As such, the mission can be an important part of the culture or atmosphere of a company.

Thirdly, the mission can serve as an important reminder of why the company exists and why its people's actions are meaningful and relevant. In fact, the mission is the connection to the meaning of the organization's activities.

Research has shown that mission-based companies often perform better than their counterparts who are primarily profit-driven instead of mission-based. In an extensive study of what they term "visionary companies," or "a very special and elite breed of institutions . . . the best of the best in their industries, and have been that way for decades," authors James Collins and Jerry Porras found that companies with meaningful missions outperform similar companies who are mainly driven by profits. The authors—who studied such visionary companies as GE, Boeing, Ford, Sony, Wal-Mart, Proctor & Gamble, Johnson & Johnson, and others—concluded in their book *Built to Last: Successful Habits of Visionary Companies*, that a major reason visionary companies achieved such success was the fact that they had a core ideology, built on what they term a "core purpose" that helped "guide and inspire" the companies' people to success.

High-level core purposes of some of the visionary companies Collins and Porras researched in the study include:

- Walt Disney—to make people happy.
- Mary Kay—to give unlimited opportunity to women.
- Merck—to preserve and improve human life.
- 3M—to solve unsolved problems innovatively.

These high-level mission statements are great—simple, universal, and heartfelt. For employees who share those values, work becomes far more meaningful than working to make the shareholders another buck or two.

These missions matter because the people believe in them, and the companies truly reflect them. I've seen many cases of companies with stellar missions on paper that don't live by them. Not only do the employees recognize the gulf between the stated mission and the companies' day-to-day reality, but they are even more alienated from the company because they see its hypocrisy. Missions have to be real to be effective.

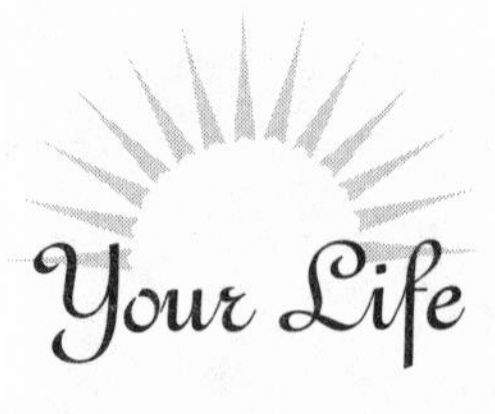

Your Life

SERVICE IS A powerful motivator. And the best thing about serving is that there are so many ways to do it! We can all serve in the specific ways that matter to us and that fulfill our own unique missions.

Accepting Your Mission

I'VE NOTICED THAT many people judge their own missions. We feel that what we love to do is not the best or most noble way to help. "It's not like we're curing cancer!" one client used to say repeatedly. OK, sure, but that doesn't mean it's not important. Every activity—in fact, every intention—is important and meaningful, and to deny that is to disrespect our own work or the work of your people. It's important for each of us to embrace your own qualities and talents instead of to judge them, and to serve the world in the best way we can—which, happily, is also the most fulfilling and fun. My clients who are doing what they believe they are meant to do seem to have no shortage of energy and find true enjoyment and meaning from their work.

Capturing Your Life's Purpose

THE MOST IMPORTANT step you will take in starting your business is aligning it with your life's purpose. Doing this will keep you focused and will help you make the most effective use of your time and energy to achieve your personal goals and find true fulfillment.

This is obviously a huge question. You may find that your answer will change over time, or that you will have more than one answer. It may, understandably, be difficult to come up with an answer at all. Here are some ways to approach it.

To define your life's purpose, first consider the following questions and answer them the best you can:

- *Why are you here?*
- *What do you have to teach, or to learn?*
- *If you could change the world in any way, what would you do?*
- *What qualities would you like to inspire in the world? What would you like to teach people?*
- *What have you done in your life that was the most fulfilling to you? In what way did it fulfill you?*
- *Can you think of other people who are making contributions that you would like to emulate in some way? Who do you most respect and why? With whom would you most like to change places?*

These are big questions, which may have many answers, and those answers may change over time. However, try to capture the answers that are true for you at this moment in time, which can inform the creation of your company.

Another way to get at your life's purpose is to call on your intuition.

> *With the intention of discovering your life's purpose, meditate every day, even if it's just for five minutes. Once you've established your intention, let go of the question and just see what comes to you. When you are finished, write down whatever came to you in a journal. Let your subconscious mind work on the question, paying attention to your dreams and writing them down in the same journal. Ask the universe for clues and information, and then watch closely. Whenever you have a thought or stumble across a piece of information that you feel may hold a piece of the puzzle, write that down in your journal too. Try on different answers and see what your heartfelt response is to it. When you hit on your life's purpose—or at least are warm—you'll know it in your heart.*

Considering Your Top Causes

WHILE YOUR COMPANY'S mission may not directly address the causes you care about, it is possible to incorporate these causes into your company, whether it's through donation of time or resources or bringing customers to special events.

One of my clients is extremely active in a major charity for a disease that impacted her family. She donates money in lieu of a holiday gift to clients. She hosts clients at major benefits for the charity. Although her company's mission has nothing to do with the charity, she donates her time and resources to the organization in ways that are integral to her company and that serve her passion for the cause.

Even if you do not work for these causes at all through your company, if these issues are important to you, then they can still play a factor in your life. You may want to develop your company to allow you enough time or resources to work for causes or organizations personally.

- *What do you care passionately about?*
- *What specific groups, causes, ideas, or concepts do you most support?*
- *How could you support these causes with your company?*
- *How could this be helpful?*

Developing Your Life's Mission

IN MY WORK with clients, I've found that some people can rattle off their missions, while others can't even begin to formulate an answer. The major difference is how much thought they've put into it at that point. Most people, with some focus, can come up with a strong answer, which applies at least to that moment in their lives.

Your life's mission is what you want to do in this life and how you want to use your specific gifts and talents to make a contribution. One client's mission is to heal children using creativity and alternative healing methods. Another client's is to inspire joy through creativity. You can be that general, or far more specific.

As you develop your life's mission statement, keep in mind that simple is always best. Go for short, sweet, and to the point. A long and cumbersome mission is less useful since it is often hard to remember.

Using your previous answers as a starting point, write a personal statement about your life's mission, in as general or specific terms as you want. You might want to do a meditation first and ask the universe for inspiration as you craft the answer to this question. See what comes, and don't force it or judge it.

How can you achieve your life's mission in terms of:

- ✦ *your significant other?*
- ✦ *your family?*
- ✦ *your friends?*
- ✦ *your coworkers and/or employees?*
- ✦ *your community?*
- ✦ *your industry?*
- ✦ *the world at large?*

How do you want to serve each of these people or groups? What is the most important thing you want to do, and how do you want to do it?

Your Company

How Your Mission Drives Your Company

YOUR COMPANY'S MISSION is its reason for being. It's the answer to the questions: Why do it? What's the point? What's the purpose?

Your company's mission will keep you on track, will guide you and inspire you and will literally raise the energy of your company and make it better. The single most important part of the work I do is to help my clients simplify and deepen their mission. It's the guiding light, the cornerstone of everything they do. It's the connection of the company with its spirit.

Your mission will help you remember why you're doing it all in the first place. It will help you build your culture by attracting people who share the same desires. It will help you motivate others when the going gets rough.

Capturing the Elements of Your Mission

YOUR COMPANY'S MISSION as I suggest you define it is a simple statement about what your company does, on a high level. It expresses what you hope to effect on a deeper level. For example, it can start with phrases like "to promote peace" or "to bring joy" with your services, product, atmosphere, attitude, etc. It may or may not also capture your business activities or products and services—sell brownies, dry clean, consult to corporations.

Some examples of missions that touch higher level purposes, as well as products and services, are:

- A child care company's mission is "to support the community by giving families peace of mind and children security by offering quality child care."

- A production company's mission is "to enlighten and inspire joy by creating magical, healing works."

This type of high-level mission may be more effective at inspiring others and reminding you of the reasons you are doing it.

Other companies focus more on their business activities than their higher level purposes, which may be more appropriate to their leaders or companies.

- A professional services firm's mission is "to help our clients achieve their goals through offering unique services with a personal touch."
- A web site design firm's mission is "to consistently delight our clients and help them meet their marketing goals through effective, tailored web site design."

These mission statements are less emotional, but they are more appropriate for these clients and their cultures.

You have to decide which approach will fit you and your company better. As long as you are clear on how the company helps you achieve your personal mission, it may not matter if you keep the company mission focused on daily activities and business results as opposed to universal, emotional goals.

You may decide to have more than one element in your mission. For example, you could have a mission for your products and services, e.g., "to support better health by providing a nutritious, tasty alternative to fast food"—and a mission for your company, e.g., "to support the community by providing jobs for the homeless." You have to decide which elements of your company's efforts are the most important to you, and which ones deserve their own separate missions—while balancing the need for simplicity.

The Keys to Creating a Successful Mission

There are five things to keep in mind when developing your company's mission:

1. Align your company's mission with your life's purpose.
2. Be specific but expansive.
3. Keep it simple.
4. Trust yourself.
5. Communicate it widely and effectively.

1. Align Your Company's Mission with Your Life's Purpose

One of the most important steps you will take in starting your own company is aligning it with your life's purpose to ensure you are making effective use of your time and energy in terms of doing what you value. That doesn't mean that your company has to be something that directly, obviously impacts the planet, like an environmental cleanup company. A closet organizing service can help people deal with and eliminate clutter, which can be metaphoric of emotional baggage. A cookie company can bring people joy with its cheerful high-quality decorated cookies. A management consulting firm can clarify the mission of its client company and help people embrace change. All of these are spiritual purposes.

Even if you choose not to use language that refers to your life's purpose, it is useful to understand how your company will help you achieve your mission. If you can't see how your company serves your own mission, you may want to rethink your reasons for doing it. I find a lack of alignment to be the most obvious warning sign that a company will turn out to be lackluster or that its creator may well lose steam before it gets legs. On the other hand, the process of aligning a seemingly unrelated company mission to the founder's life purpose offers opportunities for deepening the company into a more meaningful expression of the entrepreneur's dreams and goals.

For example, one client's life mission is to help people find and enjoy their homes. The mission of her company is to help busy people find, maintain, and sell their homes and investment properties by providing personal, dependable real estate and property management services.

How will your business help you achieve your life mission?

How will it help heal the world?

Write a statement expressing your high-level core goals for your company that is aligned with your personal life purpose.

2. Be Specific, but Expansive.

I can't tell you how many times I've read a mission statement that is so vague and high level that it becomes virtually meaningless, or, at the very least, difficult to connect with the products and services provided by the company. I encourage my clients to include specific language on what exactly their company does. It makes the connection between your company's daily activities and its high-level purpose, and it also helps explain what you do and who you are to clients or employees. Being clear and specific is always a good idea when it comes to communication.

On the other hand, your mission should be high level enough to encompass all of your company's efforts. It should cover the present and the future.

One of my clients, for example, has a technology-based company with applications that extend to many industries. To receive her initial funding, she had to focus her company on one product serving one industry. Yet her mission—to use technology to help humans reach their full potential—is big enough to encompass the myriad of ways her company can utilize their skills and knowledge to help people in a variety of industries and areas.

Refine your mission statement to also capture what your company will physically do, preferably in the context of your larger, deeper goals. And try to do it in twenty-five words or less. You may need to play with it for a while before it feels right. Remember you can't do everything with this statement—just hit the major points.

3. Keep It Simple

Remember that your company's mission needs to be short and memorable. This can be especially important as you grow. The more people you have, the more important it is to be able to effectively communicate your mission.

A complex mission can be next to impossible to communicate well, as I learned early in my career, as the person in charge of internal communications for a company with hundreds of employees. Although we had a five-pronged mission statement that was wordy and confusing, we tried hard to make up for its problems, simplifying the wording as much as we could, referring to it often, explaining it at length, even structuring our quarterly all-employee meeting presentations around its five elements.

At one point, I undertook a comprehensive survey, using questionnaires, focus groups, and interviews, to determine the effectiveness of our internal communications program. The results were humbling, to say the least. Our employees, including the vast majority of our executives, did not have adequate (in some cases any) knowledge of our mission. People were clamoring for more information on our purpose and strategy, in addition to market and customer information.

I was embarrassed but energized. I would teach them that mission! For the next year, we focused a great deal of time and effort on communicating our mission and vision and educating our employees on their role in achieving it. In every employee newsletter, the cover story focused on one element of our mission in depth. We created collateral for every employee with our vision, mission, and values on it. (In fact, I often noted with pride how many employees had the vision/mission collateral up on their walls and the laminated card in their wallets.) Each executive held meetings with his or her group to discuss how they impacted the overall company mission and to answer any questions on the company's goals.

At the end of the year, we held a corporate game show, complete with actors as hosts and significant prizes for winners. We handed out the questions in advance so people could study. One of the easier, ice-breaking questions was, very simply, "What is our mission?" Groups of ten employees had the opportunity to answer each question. To my surprise and disappointment, only one group of ten employees was able to come up with our entire five-pronged mission statement correctly. Our extraordinary efforts had an effect in that more people could probably come closer to remembering our mission, but no one really knew it. It was just too long and complex.

Is your statement as basic and simple as it can be? The shorter and more basic it is, the better chance that people will remember it. One client of mine started with a mission statement that was three paragraphs long, and ended up with this phrase: to help people relax and enjoy life through spa treatments. That says it all.

Make your statement as conversational and understandable as possible. One helpful trick is to try to explain it out loud to someone. If you trip over the words, that tells you something.

Edit your mission statement to be as simple as possible without losing its meaning. Try to edit it down to under 10 words, or as close as you can. It seems impossible, but simpler is better!

4. Trust Yourself

I once watched a client try to create her mission statement by analyzing the mission statement of her biggest competitor, highlighting words that she particularly liked, and fashioning it into her own statement. This is business insecurity. This leads to corporate identity crises. Don't do this!

It's always best to listen to your own voice and create the most honest statement you can. The energy of truthfulness is much more important than fancy words. Nobody can write a better mission statement for your company than you can, regardless of their writing or business ability or experience.

Take a look at your statement so far. Does it say what you really mean? Does it sound like you? Is it meaningful for you? If you answered no to any of these questions, work with the wording until it is something you can stand behind.

5. Communicate It Widely and Effectively

One of the very first questions that I ask when I begin working with a new client is: "What's your mission?" (It's probably the most basic question, after "What do you do?") Roughly translated, the mission question means, "What's the point?" Sadly, I rarely have the pleasure of a client's answering my question quickly or correctly, much less passionately. Of course, this means more work for me, and that I may add some value. . . . But it's a fascinating phenomenon that people are often not even aware of their own mission (and I'm including founders and CEOs in this pile).

Usually, the response to my question is a blank look, a call to a coworker ("Hey, do we have a mission? What is it? Who would know?"), or a shuffle through the annual report or corporate material to try to find the mission. One client brought me several old brochures and product sheets, which contained various divergent versions of her company's mission. She called in her top two managers to try to determine which one was current. No one knew. And this client was the CEO and founder!

If the leaders don't know, you can bet the people don't know either. Consistency and commitment are key to establishing a strong mission. You have to keep repeating it, explaining it, underscoring its importance. And you have to really believe it and live it—as do your people—for the mission to really take hold. It's work, but it's worth it.

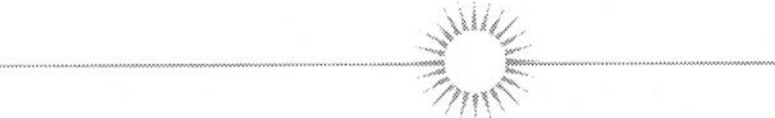

How to Lead a Group Meeting to Develop Your Company's Mission

IF YOU ARE creating a mission for a company that already exists or for a start-up with many partners or employees, you may want to include your people in the process. That is the best way to honestly capture the company's mission and to get buy-in.

Here's how you do it:

1. DECIDE WHAT YOU WANT FROM YOUR PEOPLE.

   If you want your people to be involved, decide exactly what their involvement will be. Do you want a group to work together to develop the mission as a team? Or do you want a handful of people to give input that may or may not be reflected in the final mission statement, which you plan to write on your own?

   A couple words of caution: if you include your employees, you have to be willing to cede control and truly allow the group to develop the mission together, and then live with the mission that is created. Otherwise, you could send a message to your people that you don't respect their opinions and cause anger, resentment, or hurt feelings. If you don't plan to use a mission if it does not meet your exact expectations, then you should be honest and just write it yourself.

2. CLEARLY SET OUT YOUR EXPECTATIONS IN ADVANCE AND LET EMPLOYEES PREPARE.

Once you decide how you would like others to participate in mission creation, inform the participants in advance and give them thought-provoking questions to consider before the meeting in case they want to prepare. Some people don't mind being asked to think on the spot, but others (usually introverts) do better if they are allowed to ruminate on the issues for a while before the meeting.

3. HIRE AN IMPARTIAL FACILITATOR, IF NEED BE.

If you plan to ask the group to develop the mission as a team, you may want to consider hiring an outside facilitator. As the CEO or founder, you have additional power. The person who leads or facilitates the meeting has control over the flow of information, so they also have additional power. Meetings run smoother if the facilitator is neutral and has no agenda or vested interest in how things turn out. This fact can keep the meeting on a more even keel.

A skilled facilitator can also ensure that everyone is included and that difficult participants do not derail the meeting. Of course, be aware that you may well indeed be that difficult participant. You or the facilitator should work with the group to set agreed-upon rules—and then stick to them.

A few thoughts on different processes to develop missions. Numerous consultants are available to facilitate the development of your company's mission, utilizing a variety of processes from Covey on down. I've led and attended sessions using a variety of these processes. Almost all of the ones I've experienced have been valuable. If you are considering following one of these more structured processes, you should choose the process that seems to fit best with your people. You should take into consideration the time and complexity involved, the level of structure your people need or prefer, and the style of the attending facilitator. In my experience, my less structured, organic approach can be just as effective as the more structured three-day sessions, as long as the facilitator is talented and the participants are willing and excited to participate.

4. CAPTURE ALL COMMENTS IN READABLE WRITING BEFORE NARROWING THEM DOWN.

   The first part of the meeting should be an open brainstorming session, where all ideas and answers to thought-provoking questions outlined throughout this chapter are welcomed and captured in writing, are not judged or edited, and are captured in each participant's own words. If you start out the meeting critiquing ideas, you may stifle the flow and the discussion. Capturing everything ensures that all participants feel welcome and heard.

5. CRAFT THE COMMENTS INTO ONE STATEMENT (OR SEVERAL VARIATIONS FOR A VOTE).

   After the brainstorming phase, the facilitator can help the group craft a statement, word by word or phrase by phrase. The goal is not to incorporate everything that everyone said, but to find the ideas that best capture what is true for the company. This could take some discussion, as people may stand up for or challenge different ideas. The facilitator should keep the discussion calm and respectful, even if it's passionate. You should try to work with consensus, but if that's not possible, majority rules. As always, be clear about the process and the rules before starting this phase.

6. SCHEDULE A FOLLOW-UP MEETING WITHIN A WEEK TO TWEAK AND REVISIT.

   I've noticed that, sometimes, everything looks different in the morning. After a few hours or a couple days, the information or work done at a group meeting tends to settle slightly. A follow-up meeting can allow participants to deal with any lurking, final thoughts they have had. It also takes off the pressure for finding the perfect answer in the initial meeting. (If the follow-up turns out to not be necessary, well, no harm, no foul.)

7. DEBRIEF WITH MEETING PARTICIPANTS.

   Group meetings can often be highly charged. It's easy for someone to feel undervalued, insulted, or misunderstood. That's why I've always found it useful to debrief with meeting participants after the fact to repair any small issues that could fester if not dealt with immediately. Even if this step is not necessary, participants are often thankful to be treated considerately and asked how they felt the meeting went.

8. STICK WITH THE GROUP'S DECISION IF YOU SOLICITED IT.

   It bears repeating that if you asked a group of people to work on developing the mission, you should respect their work and not change it if you don't like how things turned out. This is an all-too-common problem I've seen; the CEO or founder invites employees to participate, only to ignore the results. This is a quick and sure way to demotivate and anger employees.

Five

ENVISIONING THE POSSIBILITIES

5. develop a clear vision

A COMPANY'S VISION is the image of what that company, or its impact on others, will ultimately look like. It's the tangible outcome the people intend to create.

One of the mistakes some entrepreneurs make that takes a great toll on their lives is that they don't try to envision from the start how they imagine their companies fitting into their lives, in a basic sense. What do they hope to do every day? How does their company support that goal, or fit into their ideal lives? And, once they've figured that out, what would they like their companies to become, to ultimately look like?

The clearer and more compelling the vision is, the better. Henry Ford had a great vision for his Model T—a car in every garage. That simple phrase speaks volumes. In order to create that vision, the cars had to be affordable. There had to be a whole bunch of them. Everyone had to know about them. And even the poorest members of society had to be able to afford them. All of Ford's actions—from using soybeans in the car enamel and interior (which created demand and income for poor farmers) to mass assembly to advertising—were ways in which he sought to make his vision come true. Visions can be product-oriented or company-focused. The *product vision* offers a strong image of the ultimate goals for the company's products or services. Two of the best product visions I've heard, captured by Gregory Ericksen in his book *Women Entrepreneurs Only*, are:

- "The kind of caregiver I would want for my own mother."—Deborah Johnston, CEO and founder of Care Advantage, Inc.
- "The best coffee in the world and service with a smile."—JoAnne Show, CEO and founder, The Coffee Beanery, Ltd.

These vision statements are extremely powerful. They tell you everything you need to know. They give you a clear and compelling image without using buzzwords or vague, arbitrary statements. They are easy to communicate.

Company visions are more common, in my experience, especially in the business-to-business arena. This is the vision that usually contains some variation on the following phrase: "to be the best widget/widget consulting company in the industry/area." Using this typical variation is OK if the vision also contains specific, measurable information, and hopefully a bit of inspirational spark.

For example, one client included in her vision the popular sentiment of being the best company of its kind, a typical and vague sentiment on its own. However, we also included a definition of what that means—having the highest level of client and employee satisfaction among companies of its kind. Including the satisfaction of employees in their vision—and on a par with clients' satisfaction—was a strong message to employees about their importance to the organization. It also gave them a clear screen against which to base decisions and to determine—through measurements, no less—how well the company is living up to its vision.

Steering Toward Your Vision

VISIONS ARE ABSOLUTELY crucial for entrepreneurs. For one thing, they serve as a powerful reminder of what you want to be.

Bruce Razniewski created his company, Tall Tree Productions, with a vision of being an inspirational storyteller. His ultimate goal is to tell his own stories through writing and making films, but currently his business is primarily creating corporate videos, multimedia pieces, and meetings and events. While at the moment his vision reminds him to put the extra effort into even the most mundane of corporate projects, it is also big enough to serve as a guide for his future goals.

Another client is a web site developer whose goal is to have a second office in California, where he could work for part of the year. This goal was so important to him that he included the words "with offices in Chicago and California" as part of his vision. His vision is a great reminder of his dream and a screen against which he can develop strategies and make decisions. For example, his plans could support this vision, with tactics such as finding clients in California, developing a strong online operations so business can be done from anywhere in the world, or searching for a person or people to run the two offices when the owner can't.

Visions allow you to express to others what you're working toward in a powerful, understandable way. A clear and inspiring vision is crucial when it comes to motivating employees. Your vision is, in fact, the basis of your communications with employees, to express your dream and direction, but also to inspire and motivate. It helps you capture their imagination and focus their creativity and energy on your ultimate goals.

Partners also need to be extremely clear about their visions to make sure they are on the same page from the beginning. Partners may want to consider their vision for their company separately first or together. Either way, the important part is to have the discussion, as Martha, a client who is a marketing communications professional, can attest.

After years working in advertising and promotion for big agencies and corporations, Martha decided to change her life several years back. She had young children and needed to have more flexibility and control of her time. She started freelancing, and then decided to begin her own boutique ad agency with a partner.

All went well for two years, during which time she drummed up an enormous amount of business, even becoming agency of record for a couple of major corporations. Her partner was the designer, and they both worked out of his house. They were making a great deal of money, doing excellent work and enjoying themselves.

At a certain point, she realized that things needed to change if the company was to reach the next level. She felt they needed real office space downtown, and that she needed more help with business development and project management for the company. She shared her thoughts with her partner. He shocked her by responding that he wanted out. He wasn't willing to change his comfortable life doing graphic design from home. He had achieved his vision, which was the way things were.

Unwilling to take on the entire business by herself or to buy him out, she decided to let him buy her out instead and wash her hands of the company entirely. "If I could do it over, I would discuss our ultimate visions for the company up front," she says. "I also would have developed an exit plan. I didn't have one, so I basically had to give up the company."

Making sure you and your partner or partners share the vision for your company is crucial when you're starting out. It's hard, even when you're pretty much on the same page, but it's definitely worth the effort. It can require an incredible amount of discussion to develop a vision that everyone completely shares and believes in. This is the first major test of a partnership or an idea.

I recently considered starting a nonprofit organization with a friend, a talented advertising professional, to deal with environmental issues. We met on several occasions to discuss creating this organization and went through much of the process in this book before putting the project on hold given our busy schedules and commitment to other projects. Our mission was to educate and enlighten people about environmental issues.

We decided that we would gather the best advertising people in the industry who cared about the environment to create effective, top-quality ad campaigns that would concisely, dramatically and engagingly make the points about issues that the media seemed to be ignoring.

Then we decided to create an educational web site instead, and we began to gather research material about a variety of environmental issues. Then we decided we wanted to get children involved in writing letters about environmental issues and turn their letters into books, or have them delivered to the White House, using PR to educate the public. Then we decided that we wanted to use our creativity in terms of art and writing to express our concerns for the environment instead of going the advertising or PR route. We envisioned holding short story contests, for example, about the endangered Great White Spirit Bear. Then we decided we cared about lots of other issues too.

Then we gave up. While we agreed on a mission, we never agreed on a cohesive vision of what our organization would actually be or do within which to focus our energies. The energy of the project faded, and my partner and I began to consider other possibilities for working together. Just because partners may not be able to flesh out an idea into a viable organization doesn't mean they can't be good partners! In fact, sometimes the most successful outcome of the vision discussion with partners is to put the kibosh on the project, for the moment or forever.

I did recently go into business with another partner. We were pretty much on the same page, and yet, when we started meeting, we discovered that there were several places where we needed to clarify what we believed and wanted for the company. We had the same goals, but we had slightly different ideas about how to get there. We held extensive conversations to fully express our views and hear each other.

In the end, we honed our vision to encapsulate what we both hope for our company. In our case, we were never that far apart in our visions, but it still took some serious effort to fully understand and address both of our values and concerns. However, once we were on the same page, everything else fell into place pretty easily. It's one of those "go slow to go fast" situations. Don't be frustrated if you find that you and your partners need to discuss, argue, revisit, and clarify your vision. The vision is created through this process. It's an important step.

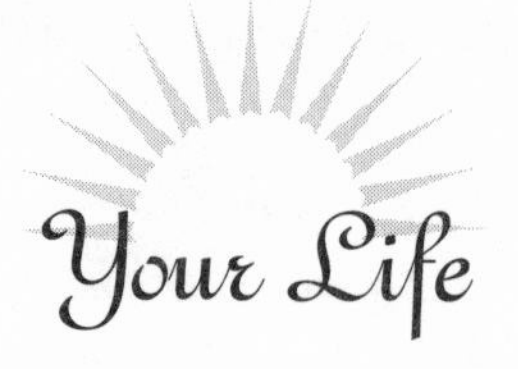

Your Life

HOW CAN YOU DEVELOP A COMPELLING VISION FOR AN ORGANIZATION UNTIL YOU HAVE A COMPELLING VISION FOR YOUR OWN LIFE—A BETTER UNDERSTANDING OF YOUR OWN VALUES, NEEDS, EXPECTATIONS, HOPES AND DREAMS? WHEN WALT DISNEY CREATED DISNEYLAND, HE WASN'T SPEAKING ABOUT AN AMUSEMENT PARK; HE WAS DESCRIBING HIS HAPPY PLACE. IT WAS HIGHLY PERSONAL AND EXPRESSED HIS VALUES, NEEDS, EXPECTATIONS AND DREAMS. MARTIN LUTHER KING GAVE VOICE TO HIS PERSONAL DREAM—A DREAM THAT ULTIMATELY IGNITED A MOVEMENT WITH A HIGHER PURPOSE, BUT ONE THAT BEGAN WITH A PERSONAL VISION. LIKE DISNEY AND KING, YOU MUST START WITH YOURSELF. ULTIMATELY, GETTING TO A VISION IS ABOUT BEING BRUTALLY HONEST ABOUT WHO YOU ARE AND WHO YOU WANT TO BE.

— Joseph Boyett and Jimmie Boyett,
The Guru Guide: The Best Ideas of the Top Management Thinkers

OBVIOUSLY, WE CAN'T control our future by simply willing it into existence. But we can focus our intentions and our energy into creating a certain type of life. Many of our choices and decisions do not take us directly toward our ideal life but actually pull us away from it. And many of us may not even have a clear idea of what we'd like our lives to be like in the future, perhaps because we've never consciously thought about it or focused on it, or because we don't believe we can actually ever have that ideal life.

When I first incorporated this part of my process—asking clients to develop a vision for their life in the future—I noticed that sometimes people were a little leery of it. However, once they get into it, they don't want to stop! Even people who insist they never dream about the future seem to come up with unbelievable detail about their visions when they commit to the idea.

Following a Life Vision

IMAGINING WHAT YOU want can help you achieve it, because your intentions can start to lead you in the direction that you want to go.

It's often difficult to discern to what degree a vision is actively created or passively received. Sometimes, though, an unexpected vision or image can be so powerful that it is undeniably life altering.

Renowned psychiatrist Viktor Frankl describes the impact of a vision of his future life that he had during a particularly difficult moment in a Nazi concentration camp when he was nearing the end of his rope. In his book *Man's Search for Meaning*, Frankl writes, "Suddenly I saw myself standing on the platform of a well-lit, warm and pleasant lecture room. In front of me sat an attentive audience on comfortable, upholstered seats. I was giving a lecture on the psychology of the concentration camp! . . . I succeeded somehow in rising above the situation, above the sufferings of the moment, and I observed them as if they were already of the past." This vision helped sustain him through almost unbearably difficult times—and no doubt gave him the idea for his life's work, which he delivered on in spades.

One friend of mine, a filmmaker, had a dream in which she experienced a clear vision of her future Hollywood career. She actually saw herself on a set, doing what she loved. It felt real and powerful to her, and she said she felt a newfound confidence and sense of calm about her career from that point forward.

Learn from Your Vision

OFTEN WHEN I take clients through the powerful exercise of creating their life visions, it feels almost like a guided meditation. As I ask them more detailed questions, the information and details that come through frequently amaze me, and often even surprise the client.

I had one such experience with Lisa Holmes of Whimsy City. She had previously expressed concern that the organization might distract her from writing or from seeking out collaborators for her own creative projects. As I took her through this exercise, however, an interesting thing happened.

Lisa was relating the details of her typical ideal day, which took place in L.A. and included a walk on the beach, writing, meetings with collaborators, lunch with friends, more writing, and a quiet dinner with her husband. After dinner, she imagined going to a benefit she was throwing for Whimsy City.

Surprised, she described a beautiful building recently built to house Whimsy City, including its lobby, hallways, classrooms, and theater. She told me about the reception, which was filled with industry bigwigs and potential collaborators. Lisa also described the teachers and volunteers who ran the program, the way the program worked, even the T-shirts with her logo on it. Never one to miss that kind of opportunity to reduce my own workload, I asked her, "What does the logo look like?" She immediately answered, "It's yellow. It has a drawing of a little kid. I'm surprised it's yellow—I'd never have chosen that—but it looks pretty cute." She went on to describe it in further detail.

The information that came through that session addressed and allayed her fears, and also gave her valuable ideas and input that she used to develop Whimsy City.

Make Sure Your Life and Business Visions Connect

THE PROCESS OF envisioning the ideal life led one client to actually change her idea for her company. Her life vision actually led her in an entirely different direction. Julia came to me after leaving her sales career in search of one that would be more fulfilling to her. As she pondered her options, she had gotten her real estate license and was managing several residential properties that she and her husband owned. Julia decided to start her own company, and came to me for help creating and marketing a property management business for small residential properties.

She had an opportunity to bid on a local project—a seventeen-unit condo association that needed a property manager—so she had an immediate need for a brochure and presentation. As we worked together to develop these, I noticed her lack of energy and ambivalence about the company. Once the marketing materials were complete, I took Julia through the personal assessment phase and the development of her personal mission.

Her personal assessment showed a passion for fitness and health, beautiful surroundings, relaxation, and healing. Her mission was to inspire people to see the beauty around them and in them. I could find almost no connection between who she was and what she wanted to do, but I decided not to address it at that point and see how things unfolded.

We moved on to the personal vision phase. The life that she desired also seemed not to fit with the property management company. I asked her to describe her ideal, fantasy life, and she came up with several, from being a rock star in San Francisco to a photographer in Paris to a jewel thief like Catherine Zeta-Jones in the movie *Entrapment*! (Imagination is always helpful because our fantasies can hold important lessons and keys for us.) Although these were clearly fantasies, each one offered important insights on what Julia wanted from life—leisure time, creativity, ability to travel, beautiful surroundings, an emphasis on fitness, excitement. Finally, as I was about to change my line of questioning, Julia said, "Oh, there's one more thing. I've always wanted to own a spa."

She went on to describe exactly what the spa would look like, the services and products she would provide, and the experience of her clients. Surprising herself with the level of detail she could see, her face lit up with that energy that had been missing from her flirtation with property management—passion. "I feel like I've had an epiphany," she said. "I feel like this is it, and it is really possible."

Although Julia had lots of reasons why the spa would not be feasible, she was excited and could accept it as a possibility down the line. So what about the property management company? Her energy came crashing to a halt. Julia decided that she could handle doing the property management company, knowing it was a temporary thing and a way to generate the money to start her spa.

That night, Julia and I called and e-mailed back and forth with ideas for the name of her spa, innovative services she could offer, and other details. I was caught up in her enthusiasm! By the time she presented to the condo association for the property management project, she realized that she had no desire to do it even as a temporary phase. She decided to abandon the property management company and begin work on the spa project right away, with energy and enthusiasm. Her spa's mission is to help people feel beautiful, special, and pampered through therapeutic massage, spa treatments, yoga and dance. It aligns with her personal mission perfectly.

Developing Your Life Vision

YOUR IMAGINATION IS crucial in developing your life's vision. This is the realm of wishes and fantasies, so try to play with it and enjoy.

Imagine yourself in five years, living your ideal life. What do you do in a typical day, from the time you wake up to the time you go to bed?

Where are you living? Who is around you? What is your home like? How is your physical state? What is your work environment like? Write in as much detail as you can about your day and your life.

If you have trouble doing this, describe your fantasy life or lives, in as much detail as you can.

Now move ahead ten or twenty years, asking yourself the same questions and capturing a typical day in your ideal life.

Now write at the end of each document, "This or something better," and enlist the help of the universe.

Your Company

YOUR COMPANY VISION should be an inspiration. It should never constrain you but instead should be a dream on the horizon that you want to reach. Your vision doesn't even have to be your ultimate goal—it can change. It can represent what you want to achieve in this phase of your company. It should motivate you, not scare the pants off you. You can always change or expand it as you go.

Your company's vision differs from your personal vision in that it should be short and simple so that it is easy to grasp and communicate. How short? One line should suffice.

While a common mistake in developing a mission is making it too complicated, the most common mistake in developing a vision is making it so vague as to be meaningless. What does it mean to be superior, world-class, excellent? And what about being number one? Number one in terms of what criteria? You have to define what you mean in clear, graspable terms.

Developing Your Company's Vision

TAKE THIS OPPORTUNITY to imagine your ideal future. In a perfect world, what will your business be? Let yourself think big. Sky's the limit. If you don't reach for it, you probably won't get it. By the same token, don't feel pressure to envision a global chain of European bakeries when all you really want is one successful scone shop in your small town, or a line of frozen scones sold in a local supermarket. Remember what success means to you, and that running your business is only a part of your life. Listen to your dream, and if your critical mind kicks in, just tell it to pipe down!

What will your company look like in five years? Ten years? What kinds of products and services are you offering? What kind of success are you having? What do your customers say about you? What are your offices like? How many employees do you have? Which of your needs and desires is it fulfilling? How is it enabling you to enjoy your passions?

Capture your ultimate, general company vision in twenty words or less.

Now edit your vision down to ten words or less! Remember, simpler is better.

Does your company vision fit within your life's vision? In what ways is it aligned? In what ways does it fall short? How can you align it to better fit within your life's vision?

How to Communicate Your Vision

IT'S IMPORTANT THAT your people share in your company vision. Visions often seem remote and unreal, but there are ways you can help make them more accessible to your people and encourage them to share in it.

1. EXPLAIN THE VISION IN REAL TERMS.

   The vision itself should be clear. However, you can elaborate on that vision with stories and examples of what that vision means. For example, what does it mean to be the services firm with the most satisfied clients in the city? Do you have an example of the lengths to which a client has gone to work with you over a competitor? Any story that provides a concrete example of the vision, once achieved, can be helpful in making it real to people.

2. FIND A SYMBOL OR LOGO THAT REPRESENTS THE VISION (AND BE SURE TO EXPLAIN IT).

   Bruce Razniewski of Tall Tree Productions has a beautiful tree for his logo, a reminder of the tree he used to climb as a child, in which he would daydream and create magical stories. The tree is a symbol of the magic of storytelling; his vision is to be an inspirational storyteller through film productions. In one direct mail, Bruce included a beautiful leaf to symbolize that magic.

   Ellen runs a production company, currently working on corporate productions, but with the ultimate vision of working in more creative fields, including film. Her logo includes a reel of film, a pen, and a paintbrush, which serves as a reminder of her vision for the creative direction of her dreams for her company in the future.

   Another client of mine had created a beautiful logo several years before that symbolized her vision. The meaning of every shape, line, and color of the logo all told part of the story, adding up to her complete vision. It was a great idea. I asked several of her employees if they could explain it to me.

They couldn't. If you have a great logo or symbol, make sure to explain it to people—clearly and often—to ensure the symbol is working for you.

3. ENCOURAGE PEOPLE AND DEPARTMENTS TO IMAGINE AND ARTICULATE THEIR ROLE IN THE VISION AND WHAT IT MEANS TO THEM.

One large company with which I worked had a very strong vision for itself in the future that included expanding its services to a much larger industry than the one it currently served. As an exercise, we asked every department to come up with its own functional vision to support the overall vision. What would each department have to do differently to support the overall vision? How would it need to change? How would it have to expand its functions? What would it look like? The exercise unearthed some great ideas and thoughts for the future, and caused employees to think about how they would each be impacted and how they would have to change to help the company reach its vision.

Leading with Values

6. be true to your values

INTEGRITY IS THE cornerstone of business because business is based on trust. Trust between you and your employees, your clients, your suppliers, your partners, the media, and the community. If trust is broken, it's awfully hard to recover.

Integrity is one of those bottom-line, deal-breaking kinds of requirements. While you can emphasize and encourage specific values, teach laws and regulations, and communicate your expectations, you cannot teach someone integrity. You can only hire people whom you believe have it and separate yourself from those who don't.

One of the less obvious ways we determine the integrity of a company is by assessing what the company stands for, and how well it lives up to its values as we understand them.

Character

YOUR CHOICES AND actions help define who you are. They illuminate your character. You can talk till you're blue in the face about your values, but they're meaningless if you do not live up to them.

Companies have character, too. The culture and spirit of the company reflects its character, as do its processes, procedures, and interactions with the outside world. And all of that comes from its shared core values.

The core values of a company are a key factor in its identity. They are the handful of values or guiding principles that are at the very heart of the company, that are essential to its very spirit.

These values make the company what it is, and they are a major part of what each person agrees to live by, which joins them together in a meaningful way. This meaning is what drives many employees, and it is the most effective way for leaders to motivate them.

Companies who share strong core values are more successful than those who don't, according to Terence Deal and Allan Kennedy, who compared extraordinary companies to their competitors in several different industries in their book *Corporate Cultures: The Rites and Rituals of Corporate Life.* Deal and Kennedy concluded from their research that outstanding companies focus significantly on their values. The authors identified three common characteristics of these companies: "1. They stand for something; 2. Management focuses on and communicates these values; 3. everyone in the company shares them."

Values-Based Organizations

SOME COMPANIES TAKE their values to an even higher level. These values-based companies elevate their values to the highest level of importance. One major feature of values-based organizations is that their values are part of the way they do business, down to their operational processes and what they do with their profits.

Two recent, prominent examples of this kind of company are The Body Shop and Ben & Jerry's. They do more than give away part of their profits to good causes. By doing things like buying brownies baked by homeless people, insisting on using dairy products from family farms who pledge not to use certain chemicals, not animal testing, or having brushes put together by underemployed groups of people in other countries, these businesses go far beyond charity. They actually build their values into their activities.

Such companies often establish extremely loyal customer bases and employee teams who are willing to pay more or get paid less, in some cases, to associate themselves with this type of company. Just as creating your own company is an act of self-expression, so is choosing to align yourself with a company by working for them or buying their products.

Ben & Jerry's Social Mission:

- We have a progressive, nonpartisan agenda.
- We seek peace by supporting nonviolent ways to resolve conflict.
- We will look for ways to create economic opportunities for the disenfranchised.
- We are committed to practicing caring capitalism.
- We seek to minimize our negative impact on the environment.
- We support family farming and other sustainable methods of food production.

From *Ben & Jerry's Double-Dip*,
by BEN COHEN and JERRY GREENFIELD

The Body Shop Principles:

- Dedicate our business to the pursuit of social and environmental change
- Creatively balance the financial and human needs of our stakeholders: employees, customers, franchisees, suppliers and shareholders
- Courageously ensure that our business is ecologically sustainable: meeting the needs of the present without compromising the future; meaningfully contribute to local, national and international communities in which we trade, by adopting a code of conduct which ensures care, honesty, fairness and respect.
- Passionately campaign for the protection of the environment, human and civil rights, and against animal testing in the cosmetics and toiletries industry
- Tirelessly work to narrow the gap between principle and practice, whilst making fun, passion and social care part of our daily lives.

From *Business as Unusual*, by ANITA RODDICK

Values Can Be Shared by Very Different People

DEVELOPING A COMPANY based on shared values does not mean hiring people who have all of the exact same values, qualities, and points of view. It just means ensuring that you hire and keep people who share certain core values that are fundamental to the company's identity. People who share core values can vary widely in terms of personality, qualities, and skills. They can even vary widely in terms of the overall set of values they each hold. What is important is the intersection of shared core beliefs.

Very different people can unite within a culture, if a subset of their values intersect as shared values. That doesn't mean people don't have other values—just that they are not the most relevant part of the culture.

It's all about context.

I once produced large meetings for a major company, which were attended by key managers, executives, and major customers and suppliers. These meetings lasted several days and were filled with lots of hard work, discussions, and brainstorming sessions with customers, strategic reviews, and lectures by top management thinkers. They were based on a theme, and were opportunities for all involved to learn from experts and interact with each other to shape the future of the company.

One year, our focus was on growth. I had brought along a video crew to film the meeting, along with a comedian to spontaneously interview attendees at breaks and then create short videos to open the next day's meeting.

Late one night, we were editing the video for the following morning. The comedian had asked meeting attendees the question, "What do you need to grow?" We had strung together a series of shots in the video, comprised of executives and managers passionately giving answers, such as: "capital," "customers," "innovative ideas," "global expansion," "opportunities," "great people," "vision," "teamwork," etc.

We went back to the raw footage to find one more answer to complete the segment. We watched as the comedian approached a carefree, tanned couple frolicking in the resort gardens in the bright sunshine (while the rest of us toiled inside).

"Who are *they*?" I asked suspiciously.

"Some people in the garden," the comedian said with a shrug.

On the video footage, he asked the woman (who may as well have been wearing a white flowy dress and flowers in her long, blonde hair), "What do you need to grow?"

"Oh!" she said, wide-eyed. "Love!"

"And you?" he asked the young man beside her.

"Yes, love," the man said, earnestly. "Love is the answer."

The couple turned to each other as if on cue and smiled beatifically.

The editor froze the tape. We all exchanged glances.

"Kill it," said the editor.

Half-joking, I said, "I think we should keep it."

Ultimately, we decided to put it last in the sequence and to flash the words "Not from our company" over their heads during their beatific smile.

The editor jumped on it, and the result was brilliant. Punchy from no sleep, we laughed ourselves silly at the juxtaposition. I decided to keep it in. And the crowd loved it.

Context. It wasn't cynical; instead, it was a reminder of a larger world out there, and it gave us a chance to laugh at ourselves.

Now, my point here is not that my colleagues were cold, hard-hearted executives. Far from it. In fact, many of them were loving, family-oriented, and compassionate people. In a different context, perhaps a family picnic, many of us may well have answered the comedian's question, "Love," and smiled beatifically. But that was not the context in which we were joined, and it did not overtly reflect the values we shared in our union.

When Your Values Clash

FROM AN INDIVIDUAL perspective, sharing core values with the company that employs you is also crucial to well-being and satisfaction. If you've ever worked for a company with core values that do not match your own (or with no core values at all), you probably have experienced how frustrating and draining it can be.

I briefly worked on a branding project with a large multinational corporation. From the moment I walked in the door, I sensed that the culture was not a good fit for me, but I couldn't tell how deep the discrepancy went. I never detected any meaningful core values that I could get behind. In fact, there was never any talk of values at all. To make matters worse, the people I worked with were constantly warning me about the many "bad people" they worked with in the company! Teamwork was obviously lacking, with people at odds with each other and all kinds of worthless political struggles that got them nowhere and stalled every project. It felt meaningless to me and was never fulfilling. I left the project as quickly as I could.

People care about the benefit of others, and most of us value working to better the world. The desire for meaningful work is a primary reason for job and career changes.

Have you ever been in a work situation where your values clearly did not match up with the values of the company for which you worked? Which values were at odds? How did it make you feel? How did you handle it?

Have you ever been in a work situation where your values completely matched up with the company for which you worked? How did you feel?

Another reason many people make job changes is for a better quality of life, and not just in terms of money. Several colleagues and clients of mine jumped the corporate ship in the past few years so they could have a better lifestyle, even if that required taking risks (not to mention pay cuts). Often, the major payoff was time. Time for families and friends. Time to pursue hobbies and dreams. Time for ourselves. Another major payoff from going out on your own is the ability to work for your *own* vision and values.

One friend of mine left an executive position at a major association to work freelance out of her home, mainly writing for web sites. She got a puppy, played golf, worked out every day, took acting classes and voice lessons, and spent time with her new husband. She was more relaxed and fulfilled than I had ever seen her in the several years I had known her.

After a couple years, she caught wind of a job working for a company that focused on one of her passions—golf. The job was particularly appealing to her because not only was it close to where she lived, but it also was dog-friendly. She could take her dog to work, and she even got pet insurance as a benefit. (One sure sign that a company values something is the fact that they're willing to pay for it!)

At the interview, she also saw that the atmosphere of the company was warm, fun and creative. Although she had not planned to take another full-time job, she left the freelance world to join this company, and she has never looked back. She certainly could have made more money elsewhere, but being able to bring her dog to work, in a positive atmosphere, was an unbeatable opportunity for her.

Another client of mine left the academic world—although she was a shoo-in for tenure the next year—because she wanted to break free of what felt to her like an outdated system and work for herself. She started a technology company.

She says, "I was working for someone else's definition of success. Everything I was doing was for someone else's vision that I felt was not well defined and was totally contrived. Now, all my efforts—even when they're not pleasant, like dealing with lawyers—it's all for a purpose that I define. Before, it was a learned helplessness. Now that I'm in control of my own destiny, the effort is less onerous because I enjoy it. And even in the moments that I don't, it's a well-defined goal and vision—one I've brought into the world of my own will."

Making major job changes based on values is not the exclusive domain of Gen X-ers and Y-ers, either. Another client of mine, a technology company, has the following core value: "getting the job done and delivering what we promise." This company has recently attracted a major, high-level talent with a world-class management consulting background in part because he liked the idea of doing more than making recommendations and passing the buck; he wanted to see the project through for clients, from planning to implementation and beyond.

Would you be willing to take more risk or make less money to accept a job working with a company that shared specific values? What would those values be?

Your Life

WE ALL HAVE our own moral code and our own values. Not all of your values will end up being core values of your company. As your company is only one way to express facets of yourself, it probably will not reflect you or your values in an exact, comprehensive way.

List your values (e.g., honesty, treating everyone equally, learning continuously, etc.). Now choose your top seven to ten values.

Write these values in the form of principles, or commandments, for yourself. Imagine you are creating your own list of commandments for how you want to live your life and interact with other people.

Make Sure You Share Values with Your Partners

IF YOU'RE PLANNING to work with a partner or partners, not only are integrity and trust paramount, but shared values are also crucial.

One client, who founded her engineering company with a partner, says she decided to work with him because they share values, including: helping others through technology; maintaining balance and time with their families; and having fun. "We're very different, but we share a general philosophy. Neither of us is in it for the money, but instead we like pursuing the challenge and helping people with the technology," she says. "And we've always said that when we stop having fun, we'll know it's over."

Values and philosophy also come into play when you choose people to invest in you or form strategic alliances. In fact, anyone you tie your future to should probably share your basic philosophy and values. One client says, "You want investors to get it and understand your vision. If we get rejected by an investor because we are not philosophically aligned, then I don't want them anyway. I don't want them to share my business."

It's a good idea to capture your own values first as an individual, and then go through the process again with your partner to explore your shared values as a team. Going through this process separately and together will help you identify where you may have differences of opinion. Believe me, you'll want to know this before you tie your future together in a partnership.

How much do your values overlap?

Which values do you share absolutely?

Which values do you not share or prioritize differently?

If your partner does not share certain of your values, how important is that to you?

Your Company

THE PEOPLE IN a company help determine its character and values. That's why it's important to be clear about the values and principles on which you'd like your company to be based. These values need to be the foundation of your recruiting, hiring, reviewing, and other people practices, not to mention communications. If you don't act as the guardian of your values, and develop the processes to inculcate and preserve them in your organization, they could get diluted.

When you are in the process of creating a company, it's important to determine your principles and build on them, while recognizing that you can not control what your values will actually end up being. You may need to occasionally take stock of the state of your values, and let them evolve as your company grows.

So how do you ensure that what you'd like your company's core values and guiding principles to be will be embraced and shared by the people in your company?

1. Create a Values Statement
2. Hire people who share your core values and part with those who don't.
3. Incorporate the values in all facets, processes, and systems of your company.
4. Clearly and consistently communicate your values.
5. Live by your values.
6. Share responsibility for values with employees.
7. Don't allow clear integrity violations.

1. Create a Values Statement

If you are already running a company, you can't hope to create and establish values so much as uncover authentic shared values that already exist. If you're unhappy about the state of your company's values, it probably means that you need to take a hard look at your people and make some changes, because values cannot be taught.

List the three to five values or guiding principles you are most committed to having your company live by.

2. Hire people who share your values and part with those who don't.

The values of your company should be a major part of the recruiting and hiring process. Trust me, while interviews have major limitations in terms of getting at the truth, you will nonetheless save a great deal of time if you ask potential employees about their values and communicate your company's principles from the earliest discussions forward.

Performance appraisals and reviews should also focus on how well the people exhibit the company's core values.

Develop at least three interview questions to determine a prospective employee's commitment to each of your core values. For example, if the value is teamwork, you could ask questions like:

- *How do you function on a team?*
- *What was the best experience you had working on a team?*
- *What was the worst experience you had working on a team and what did you learn from it?*

Develop at least three performance appraisal questions to ask the person's boss, coworkers, or subordinates and the person him/herself about performance relative to each of your company's core values.

3. INCORPORATE THE VALUES IN ALL FACETS, PROCESSES, AND SYSTEMS OF YOUR COMPANY.

If you value teamwork, don't just reward individuals. Reward teams, or individuals who exhibit teamwork. If you value personalized service, don't create customer processes that are impersonal, such as sending out "Dear Valued Customer" mailings. If you value innovation, develop processes to gather ideas from employees, or provide resources for ideas to be developed or tried out.

What processes can you develop to support, reflect, or reinforce each of your company's values or principles? List at least one way to institutionalize each value or principle in each of the following areas:

- *hiring*
- *training*
- *employee communications*
- *performance appraisals*
- *rewards*
- *celebrations*
- *benefits*
- *operational processes*
- *sales promotions*
- *customer communications*
- *community service*

4. CLEARLY AND CONSISTENTLY COMMUNICATE YOUR VALUES.

In order to clearly communicate your values, you should use simple words to explain simple concepts. You should give examples of the values in action. You should consistently and repeatedly discuss the values. And most important, you should remember that we communicate in lots of ways far more potent than words—with our tone, with our energy and attention, and, finally, with our actions (see next point).

Develop at least one example of each of your core values and principles in action.

Develop at least one example of each of the core values or principles being broken.

5. Live by your values.

The main point here is to walk the talk. If you say you value diversity, don't hire a bunch of people who look and think exactly like you. If you say you value balancing work and family, don't hold meetings on Saturday.

Of course that doesn't mean you have to be perfect. Nobody is. But if you fall short, you have to make amends. When you catch yourself not living your values, you apologize and do better next time. To live up to your values and have credibility, you have to recognize your shortcomings and make an honest effort to rectify the situation.

Develop at least one goal for achieving each value or principle. For example, if the principle is "integrity," the goal could be total compliance with all laws and regulations. If it is "continuous innovation," the goal could be to develop and/or launch a certain number of new or improved products each year.

6. Share responsibility for values with employees.

Explain to employees what it means to do their part holding up the values. Give them a role in maintaining the company values, for example by asking them to do 360-degree performance appraisals, rating their coworkers, bosses, and subordinates on their success in reflecting each value.

7. Don't allow clear integrity violations.

Inadvertently falling short of certain values is one thing. Cheating or stealing is yet another. Certain types of deliberate activities are never acceptable. If you let certain things go on unpunished, you will create an atmosphere that allows dishonesty and you will lose credibility.

Develop a list of integrity violations that are grounds for dismissal. (Always check this kind of document with a lawyer before sharing it with employees.)

Explain as clearly as possible, using realistic examples, activities that are not allowable. Use clear, not legalistic, language.

Familiarize yourself with legal and accounting issues.

When it comes to integrity, you need to be vigilant. Part of your responsibility is to develop the knowledge you need to work within laws and regulations. You have to educate yourself and your people. To do this effectively—and to protect yourself and your company—you will no doubt need to have a lawyer and accountant you can trust. Business and tax laws are complicated and often counter-intuitive, and ignorance is never an excuse.

How much legal, accounting, and insurance advice you need depends on you, although I always recommend erring on the side of caution. I know myself—my brain shuts down when legal minutiae or taxes on any level are discussed in my presence. I have an accountant who does my books and a lawyer who keeps my papers up to date. Both keep on top of me and remind me whenever anything is due. You may be good at staying on top of all the bureaucracy involved in running a business—I am not. Protect yourself. It's worth the money to know you're playing by the rules.

That's not to say you can let the details slide by. Even with accounting and legal advice you trust, you still have to understand your responsibilities in at least a general sense, and you have to know where your money is. It's helpful to buy a software package to help you keep your company's books straight, but I recommend also getting help from an accountant or other consultant to ensure you are using it correctly.

When hiring an accountant or lawyer, make sure you check out their references or find them through a qualified referral. Of course, keep in mind that anyone given as a reference is probably an extremely happy client who is going to be complimentary. You should cover your bases beyond just references. Call the American Bar Association or Better Business Bureau. Meet them, go to their offices, and be sure to listen to your intuition. When you hire people, check out their advice with a third party, perhaps a friend or relative who is a lawyer or an accountant or fellow entrepreneur with more experience, to see if the advice you're getting makes sense.

How to Communicate Your Values to Your People

YOUR PEOPLE SHOULD not only know what your values are, but they should also understand your expectations about their roles and responsibilities in propagating those values.

1. **USE ENGAGING STORIES TO ILLUMINATE EACH VALUE.**

   Value statements in themselves can be vague or can be interpreted in different ways by different people. You can effectively communicate what you mean to your employees by telling them engaging stories that explain each of your values in a deeper, more emotional way. You can, for example, tell stories about someone who manifests your values in the sense that you mean it, whether the main character is you or Michael Jordan. If one of your values is teamwork, for example, use an example of how your people went beyond the pale to work together to make something happen. One of my clients once passed out the book *Sacred Hoops* by Phil Jackson as a

great example of a team in which every person matters and has a role. Another client hosted an improvisation workshop with exercises focusing on teamwork so his people would get an even deeper sense of how working as a team with their coworkers could feel and help them succeed as a group.

Telling personal stories about how you learned the importance of one of your values the hard way—by not getting it right, with bad results—is one way to avoid being preachy. Humor is another great way to engage people without putting them off. If you do not have any personal examples, telling stories about well-loved figures (even unknown but interesting characters can work) will help you get your point across in a way that other people care about.

Asking employees to share stories of how another person in the company lives your company values is a nice way to get people even more engaged. One way to do this is to give out an award for values, based on nominations written by employees about each other. This strengthens the culture through drawing on emotional connections between people, in the words and with the initiative of employees, but with the support of the leaders.

Write down at least one interesting, universal but personal story for each value.

2. Recognize the importance of symbolic gestures.

Think of ways you can incorporate each of your values into your daily routine. If one of your values is valuing the family, make it a habit to ask your people often about their family members—then remember what they say and follow up! Send flowers for an employee's anniversary or child's graduation. Have a family picnic for your employees. Do something special on "Bring Your Child to Work Day."

List one or two symbolic things you can do to reinforce each value.

3. EXPLAIN YOUR ACTIONS IN TERMS OF THE VALUES.

One manufacturing client plowed the parking lots of his office and factory himself because it was so much cheaper than hiring a company to come and do it. When I heard leaders in the company telling others how the owner used to do this, they always added "because he has a deep respect for the customer's money." In this context, this example becomes a powerful anecdote for communicating a value, instead of perhaps being seen as a way to save a buck. The sacrifice and effort on the owner's part helped keep employees' morale high whenever pennies had to be pinched.

Make sure that your stories include a simple sentence that explains how the action represents one of your values.

Seven

Telling Tales from the Heart

7. tell your story

Storytelling is an ancient and fundamental form of communicating. We've learned through stories all of our lives, and we are still engaged by stories. It's an extremely effective way of passing on culture and history. While we may no longer have tribal storytellers, we certainly have movies and TV shows and novels and songs—all different ways of telling stories.

Storytelling is a way of communicating not only what you do, but who you are—your spirit, soul, and personality. Implicit within every story is a wealth of information.

As an entrepreneur, you'll find that you'll be telling your story over and over, to many different people. Those include:

- Investors
- Clients and prospects

- Recruits and employees
- Suppliers
- Partners
- Media
- Your industry

These parties will not necessarily be interested in the same information or they may prefer to receive information in different ways. Nonetheless, your communications will be most effective if your overall messages are unified and consistent, even when they are varied and targeted to different audiences. Consistent messages build trust and credibility, and also leverage your brand and/or identity. The basic story and key messages will remain the same.

Your basic stories and key messages are the foundation of your communications. In this chapter, you will develop the content that you will share with the world about who you are and what you do.

Your Life

AS A COURAGEOUS entrepreneur, your life can be an inspirational example to others. As a leader, your passion can be a motivating, magnetic force for employees, partners, investors, and clients. As a human being, reflecting on your journey is a great way to get insight into yourself and remember who you are and why you're doing this.

Your personal stories may one day inform your company's culture. Often, the founder or leader of a company becomes a significant part of the brand or company's identity. Virgin's Richard Branson, Microsoft's Bill Gates, and Ben Cohen and

Jerry Greenfield of Ben & Jerry's are great examples of this. It's nearly impossible to think of the brand separately from the owners. When Richard Branson flies a balloon into the ocean or wears a dress, it enhances and reinforces Virgin's fun and adventuresome image.

One client, Ashlee, who recently started a dog training business, shared with me many stories about her lifelong affinity for dogs and her ability to reach and calm troubled pups, even as a small child. In the early stages of developing her company's identity, I told a few friends with new puppies about her business. They had already lined up training with more established, larger firms, but they were swayed when I shared her stories. I wasn't trying to convince them to change their plans, either—I was just telling her stories because I thought they were interesting. Her natural ability with dogs and her passion for working with them were enough to override the credibility of established firms in my friends' eyes. Through the stories' authenticity and honesty, they saw her passion and connected with her enough to trust her with their puppies.

Personal stories also can convince investors or foundations to take a chance on you. Investors are looking not only for good business concepts in markets with good potential, but also for the right people. They want to know who you are and why they should trust you with their money. While they don't want to read long, rambling stories, it is useful to include in business plans or grant applications personal stories about the founder and management team that illustrate their passion, talents, and qualities as they specifically relate to the issue, product, or service at hand.

And last but not least, the best reason to capture your story in the early stages is for you. It is a great way to look deeply at why you are undertaking this project, how it fits into your life as a whole, and the personal meaning it has for you. If you choose, you can adapt and use your story in your business plan, grant applications, marketing efforts, employee communications, advertising, customer relations, or public relations efforts.

I often ask clients to tell me or write the story of how they first were inspired to start their organizations. This exercise is very grounding and can be a great way to anchor your efforts to start your business in what matters to you and what touches you as a person. Here is one prime example:

WHIMSY CITY

by Lisa Holmes

Before I launch into the story about the Whimsy City Theatre Program's inception, I first have to introduce an eight-year-old boy named Bobo.

Bobo is a whip-smart kid who likes video games, Nike gym shoes and playing basketball with the other kids in our tutoring program on the Southwest side of Chicago. I was Bobo's tutor, and in that role, I was supposed to be teaching Bobo about reading, geography, spelling, math and all the other lessons a kid in the second grade would need. But it was Bobo who ultimately turned out to be the teacher in the equation—because he taught me the value of truth when it comes from the heart.

"Out of the mouths of babes" is what they say. And in my and Bobo's case, nothing could be closer to the truth.

It was a typical Saturday morning when a visiting theater troupe came to lead the children in a theatrical exercise of reenacting the entire history of African Americans. No small undertaking for a few hours' time, some makeshift costumes of robes and wigs, and twenty children with little-to-no theater training. The kids were hyped up on sugar. We had just served the 10:30 a.m. snack that Bobo always hungrily anticipated. I got the feeling that Bobo didn't have much to eat. Before snack time, his concentration was nil, he'd bounce his knees and look around the room, frantically, asking me for the time. Then, during this sacred fifteen minutes, Bobo would stuff cookies and grapes into his mouth with reckless abandon. What he couldn't finish, he'd shove deep into his pockets for later.

After snack time, he'd regain his focus and return to the bright, calm kid we knew him to be.

I was excited to see how this theater troupe would engage the children. As a writer myself, specifically a playwright, I have a passion for theater and all it entails. In fact, that very evening, I was looking forward to the play my husband and I would be attending at one of the largest and most well-respected theaters in Chicago.

Little did I know that the show I was about to see in our dilapidated tutoring space could easily rival anything I'd ever see in a more glamorous venue.

The troupe began by dressing the kids in burlap rags and having them sell each other on auction blocks. Half the children got to play plantation owners and the other half were slaves. These children moved through their own history, acting out their escape to the North led by Harriet Tubman, and Rosa Parks' monumental bus ride. The kids were really getting into it, assuming voice changes for specific characters, acting out the parts with bold, dramatic gestures.

The tutors, most of us white, stood on the sidelines with tears in our eyes, watching these miraculous African American children create heartfelt, passionate theater.

When they got to the life of Martin Luther King, each child was encouraged to stand tall on a chair and repeat part of Dr. King's inspiring "I have a dream" speech, only they were asked to fill in the famous speech with their own particular dream.

The first child climbed up on the rickety old chair. Projected behind her on a screen was an archival photograph of Dr. King behind a podium, with his fist raised proudly. She spoke boldly, "I have a dream . . . that people all over the world can get along with each other peacefully." A noble request for a six-year-old. We were all impressed. The next little one bounded up. "I have a dream . . . that there will be no more sickness." Another impressive request from someone so young. It went on like this through the rest of the children, each one creating his or her utopia through a dream. When it got to Bobo, the room fell silent. He was the last child to speak. We held our breath in anticipation of the grand finale. Before climbing up on the chair, he looked behind him, perhaps for inspiration from his wise older brother, Dr. King.

Bobo finally summoned the nerve to speak. His dream was shaky at first, but became stronger and bolder with each syllable. "I have a dream . . ." he blurted out, ". . . that all mothers and fathers can feed their children."

We were silent. Stunned. Awed. Bobo had spoken truth from his heart. He was starving. And he was honest about it.

Bobo, and the other nineteen children, had acted on the passions in their souls. Their performances were not acted out, memorized lines, but instead the stuff from which hearts are made. We didn't need a four-hundred-seat proscenium stage. We didn't need SAG or AFTRA or the Writers Guild. Props and costumes were minimal. There wasn't any elaborate lighting—just a single, dangling forty-watt bulb hanging over our heads.

Hopefully Whimsy City will influence several children, or even just one. I'd like to let kids know they can actually work in the theater and film professions. Maybe if they get a jump-start, they'll have longer, more successful careers. Maybe a child or two will learn to value life, and self, through the art of theater. Maybe a child can learn about the value of self-expression and the importance of heartfelt storytelling.

Write at least two or three pages about how you decided to start this company and what it means to you. Answer the following questions:

How does this company fit into your life story?

How did you get interested in this field?

What led you to start this company?

What has your journey been to this point?

Why is this company, issue, product, or service important to you?

Your Company

Creating Your Company's Messages and Stories

I FIND THAT it's most effective to begin with your overall story and then adapt the way you tell it to various audiences. I always start with the key messages of the company. Your key messages are simple sentences that summarize the essential facts about your company. These key messages should be implicitly or explicitly communicated in everything you do.

Key messages may include:

- What you do
  EX.: Lily's Pies bakes and delivers freshly made pies.
- Where you do it
  EX.: Lily's Pies serves the greater Milwaukee area.
- Who you do it for
  EX.: Lily's Pies provides pies to restaurants and institutions.

You can combine these messages, of course. For example: Lily's Pies bakes and delivers freshly made pies to restaurants and institutions in the greater Milwaukee area.

- How you do it (what makes you unique)
  EX.: Lily's Pies uses fresh ingredients and guarantees delivery within twenty-four hours of baking.
- Who you are
  EX.: Lily's Pies is a local, family-owned business operating out of our family home and using our grandmother's secret recipe.
- Your key values
  EX.: We offer warm hospitality, reliability, honesty, and granny-approved quality.

- Your personality, including key characteristics or qualities
  EX.: Lily's Pies is friendly, trustworthy, and old-fashioned when it comes to quality and service.

- Your brand features and benefits
  EX. (Benefit): Lily's Pies are the best-tasting pies you've ever had, having won number one in the National Apple Pie Contest for five years running and in numerous local and regional baking contests.
  EX. (Feature): Lily's Pies uses only fresh ingredients and no chemicals or preservatives.

You can use these simple key messages to craft your communications, including your company profile, press releases, and customer brochures. You can save a lot of time if the key people in a company can agree to the key messages up front before they are applied to web site copy, brochures, or other pieces. And the key messages can be handed to anyone who is working on your communications, including your ad agency, PR people, marketing people, etc., so they will all be on the same page.

If one of your key messages is, "We are warm, friendly, and old-fashioned," you probably will never use those words explicitly in your communications. However, those key adjectives can be communicated through design, color, and tone.

Once you have created these messages, you have to keep them alive. You can't just write them down and forget about them. It is important to repeat them and continuously reinforce them in ways appropriate to your audiences. So let's start with your key messages.

Develop five to ten key messages that capture the most important facts about your company.

Then, write a short, comprehensive profile of your company. This should encapsulate who you are, what you do, and the other basics of your story. It does not need to incorporate all of your key messages, but it should reflect your personality if possible. For example, if your personality is to be friendly but professional, try to be warmly conversational but businesslike. If your personality is to be irreverent and fun, reflect that in your writing.

Identity Stories

A MAJOR FUNCTION of stories is to describe your company's identity and to reinforce your culture. The stories can focus on:

- Who you are—name, experiences, charismatic leader stories, company identity stories
- Your company history, including how you came into existence
- What your name means
- Success stories and case studies

An example of a famous identity story centering on a charismatic leader is the one about how Fred Smith, the founder of FedEx, wrote a college paper on the need for a new logistics system to serve industry—and got a C. As Gretchen Morgenson reports in *Forbes: Great Minds of Business,* Smith says, "Well, that's a bit of an apocryphal story. It got exaggerated, but I'm smart enough to know it was turned into a great story. And that has now become a part of the FedEx story."

In my experience, GE people often related how Jack Welch blew up a chemical plant early in his career with the company. Richard Branson's exploits, silly or adventuresome, have become a large part of Virgin's lore.

I recently worked on awards shows honoring top entrepreneurs in two cities, writing up nearly fifty profiles of the finalists in both cities. Virtually all of the entrepreneurs had some sort of identity story I could tap into—usually some variation on the hero's journey, battling huge odds and facing great challenges, and coming out on top. This is your journey! (If you don't have any great identity stories yet, just wait.)

Write an identity story about you or your company. If you don't have one yet, write a fictional story that expresses an aspect of your company or you as a leader that you aspire to achieve one day.

Naming Your Company

THE NAME OF your company carries enormous weight and offers tremendous opportunity to communicate who you are and/or what you do (preferably both). It will be a reflection of your company's personality.

Some people prefer to choose names that have meaning mainly for themselves. My accountant's company, for example, consists of three initials followed by "Financial Services." I asked him one day what they stood for, and it turns out they are the initials of his three sons—a nice reminder of why he works so hard! He's also not trying to brand his company name because his reasons for incorporating are financial, not customer-based, so it makes sense his name is more personal than externally-focused. And using a professional, rather dry-seeming name is appropriate given the fact that he's offering accounting services and is very straightforward and professional. I wouldn't be drawn to RWJ Hair Salon, but I also wouldn't trust Buzz Accounting or Fred's Bank.

When it comes to companies offering creative services, especially, personality can become an important element of the name. Not only is there a lot more freedom in that arena, but the creativity you exhibit in your name can influence your client's decision whether or not to talk to you. I'm often asked by clients to help them find web site development companies, design firms, or video production companies for specific projects, and I usually begin with a list of eight or ten places to present to the client for general reaction before culling them down to two or three companies. It's amazing how much the creativity or uniqueness of the name attracts clients early in the process, until they meet the people. And it's also amazing how often the name really reflects the personality of the people who show up to represent it!

Jim, a devoted Buddhist who owns a commercial music company, had a difficult time choosing a name at first. His competitors had impossibly hip names like Spank, Deaf Dog, and Rhythm Café—aimed at advertising creatives. This type of name did not express who he was, though. We finally came up with the name Earthborne Music, a grounded name to reflect his personality. The name is not only an honest representation of the company, but it also stands out from his competitors.

Jen Shiman of Angry Alien Productions, who also offers creative services, says, "I needed to name my fledgling business. One day, I created some sample logos for my first design portfolio using fictitious company names. As I sketched absent-mindedly, the head of an alien materialized on the page. He was cute, but he looked pissed. So I drew his body in an irritated pose, next to a phone, as if he had been waiting forever for it to ring. The name Angry Alien Productions seemed quite fitting for the logo. Eventually my fondness for the peeved alien led me to take the fictitious name and make it my own. The logo and name embody my love of creating cute and satirical characters, as well as the organic process from idea to finished artwork. Clients, vendors, and particularly cranky city workers have greeted the name with amusement. I feel exhilarated doing what I love and crafting a maverick corporate identity that dares to explore the realm of all that is wacky and silly."

The best possible scenario for a name is one that captures your vision and mission, if only for you. This is rare, but it is a beautiful thing when it happens.

As Kevin said about his Morningstar Theater Company, "The name, Morningstar, always appealed to me—even the sound of it. It represents hope after a long night, rebirth, and a guiding light. Through my own healing process as an artist and human being, I learned that I was not alone in my desires for an extraordinary life. This fueled the mission of Morningstar, to offer hope and healing through truthful and powerful productions perhaps revealing to both the audience and performers the beauty within themselves."

Here is the story of how one client came up with his company's name. This story is extremely effective because it sets up the company's vision and purpose in an engaging, emotional way.

WHY TALL TREE?

by Bruce Razniewski

When I was a young boy growing up in a rural area of America, not too long before it was overrun by suburban sprawl, my friends and I could step out of our doors and into the Secret Woods. It was an untamed place of magic, imagination, and limitless possibilities.

At the very heart of the Secret Woods was a huge tree. It was the oldest and tallest tree in the woods. On the first of its many great boughs was a tree fort. On that platform we could be magically transported to any place or any time known or unknown. We could do anything and be anybody—even ourselves. In the old tree epic adventures happened every day. We assailed impossible challenges, risked everything, played for keeps, and always got home for dinner, safe and successful.

One glorious summer morning we climbed higher than we ever had before, to the topmost branches of the old tree. Spread out before us in all directions a vast unexplored countryside beckoned. Its smoky horizons promised unlimited possibilities. On that day we knew that our adventures could go on forever. We could go anywhere we let our imaginations take us.

The Secret Woods is gone now, given way to tidy streets of splendid houses, its enchanted wilderness domesticated by the visiting crews who trim the lawns of the fastidious homes which stand where we used to play.

And the old tree?

Well, now you know where you can find it.

Write the story of how your company got its name.

How to Tell a Meaningful Story

1. CARE ABOUT IT.

   Speak from the heart. Tell us about something that matters to you. After all, if you don't care, why should we? If you do care, we'll be able to tell, and we'll care more too.

2. HAVE A MESSAGE.

   Be clear about what your major point is in telling your story and beware of going off on tangents. If it gets too complicated, you'll lose us.

3. REVEAL A TRUTH.

   Whether your story is something that actually happened to you or a fictional parable, make sure it addresses a truth that is real and meaningful.

4. USE ILLUSTRATIVE DETAILS AND EXAMPLES.

   Paint the picture with interesting details. That makes the story more rich and entertaining for your audience, and can also save time. For example, "He has a swimming pool shaped like his own head" tells us in a quick, interesting way as much as or more than, "He has a lot of money, a healthy ego, a sense of humor, and a flamboyant, eccentric style." It also leaves the judgments up to the audience.

5. BE WILLING TO PLAY THE FOOL.

   People appreciate vulnerability, and we like to root for the underdog. Tell us what you learned. That means to include what you used to think and who you used to be before something happened to change your mind. Self-deprecating humor is always very effective—people are less likely to warm up to a story about how great you are than one about how you screwed up but then grew in some way.

6. TELL ABOUT A TRANSFORMATION.

   Instead of just telling us what happened, tell us the impact it had on you or others from before it happened to well after, if possible. Take us with you on your journey (but make sure it's interesting).

7. BE GENEROUS AND GRACIOUS.
   Give credit where credit is due. If someone did something awful, don't skewer them by name. However, if others were involved and did something noteworthy in the story, acknowledge them. Be generous in your treatment (and judgment) of others—people are learning about you in this story too.

8. DETACH FROM ANY NEGATIVE EMOTIONS.
   If you are still angry or upset with someone in the story, don't let that emotion overtake your theme or your point. Audiences can be distracted by emotion like that, and negative emotions can drag our attention away from your point.

9. SAVE SOMETHING FOR YOURSELF.
   You don't have to give it all away. Leave something to subtext. Dragging your burning soul into the light is fine in many situations, but in certain business situations, maybe not so much. Less is more, much of the time, so give us a little hint at your strong emotion, let us see it . . . but don't weep and wail and tear at your hair if it doesn't fit the context. You may just make your business audience uncomfortable. Consequently, we may be intrigued at what you suggest but don't say. We like depth, and we can sense it. Audiences pick up far more than just words.

10. SAY IT IN AS FEW WORDS AS POSSIBLE WITHOUT LOSING MEANING.
    We get bored easily. Try to paint the picture as concisely as you can. If you are redundant or give too many examples, you may lose us.

11. DON'T SPELL OUT THE "CORRECT" INTERPRETATION.
    The meaning should be clear, but don't hit us over the head with it or tell us exactly how we should interpret it. Leave that up to us.

12. LEARN FROM OTHERS.
    Listen to others' stories or read fairy tales or parables from the perspective of a storyteller and an audience member. What makes this story work or not work for you? Also, practice your stories on others, and learn from their feedback about what you're doing well or what you could improve.

Eight

Connecting With Your Audience

8. adapt your messages to your audience

THE IDENTITY OF your company or enterprise does not exist in a vacuum. You can't totally create or control it, because a huge part of it is in the eye of the beholder. You can be very clear about who you are and take great pains to express yourself carefully, and yet you have little if any control over how others respond to you. God only knows what they are projecting on you or what has shaped their perspectives. All you can really do is be yourself.

You can stay essentially who you are and adjust to different contexts. You don't change as a person just because you wear jeans to a ballgame but a formal outfit to a benefit (or vice versa). You're simply expressing yourself in different environments. You probably wouldn't spontaneously give a speech at a friend's party—you'd have a conversation. And you wouldn't give the same speech to the Board of

Directors of Microsoft as to a nursery school class of four-year-old children. That doesn't mean you are being dishonest about who you are. You're just being sensitive to the audience and adapting to the situation to communicate most effectively.

Your Life

WE EXPRESS OURSELVES in many ways, often without realizing it. The way we dress, our home, our pets, our cars, our jobs, all provide clues to who we are. Sometimes the clues are false ones to throw people off the track. Sometimes they give away more than we want them to. In fact, our life is the ultimate expression of ourselves. If we are totally authentic and honest with ourselves, our lives will totally make sense. If there are areas where we are not authentic, our lives will reflect that back to us with unhappiness, discomfort, or disease.

Before we know someone, we take their self-expression at face value. People constantly judge each other based on appearances, first impressions, or actions taken out of context. We take a limited amount of information and extrapolate a reality out of it. Often, all is not as it seems. If you've ever been judged unfairly, based on something taken out of context or an uncharacteristic action, you know how painful it is to be misunderstood.

As an adult, I have often come across in first impressions as younger and more vulnerable than I am. Maybe it's the hair, who knows. All I know is, as a corporate vice president in my twenties, I had a lot of visitors asking me to get them coffee (I would, of course). And a lot of employees did not know what to make of me, and did not take me very seriously at first. As time went by, people got to know me and realized what I was really like. Of course, even years later, on occasion, newcomers still asked me to get them coffee!

Being who you are does not always translate exactly. Sometimes you have to alter the way you present yourself to make sense within a certain context. Sometimes you may choose to do that with the way you look, or you may choose to do it with the way you act in given situations. This does not necessarily mean you have to misrepresent who you are.

Are you ever misunderstood or misjudged by people? Why do you think that is?

Do you ever have to play a role or wear a uniform that feels false to you? When?

How do you express yourself in the physical world?

What do your major relationships reveal about you?

What does the way you dress say about you? Do you wear clothes that you love? Are your clothes a good clue to the real you?

What is your home like? Does it reflect the state that you're in at this point in your life? Is it an authentic expression of who you are?

Your Company

Connecting Through Communications

Compelling content is necessary but not sufficient to having great communications. Having a great story is meaningless if you don't reach a listener. You need to effectively express yourself to the rest of the world. We've already developed content; now we need to talk about delivery of those messages.

How do you communicate to the outside world in a meaningful way who you are, what you stand for, and the value you provide? Your key messages, personality, and look and feel should all be implicitly or explicitly expressed to the world at large, through every interaction you have with customers. And your stories and messages will be most effective if you are able to establish a heartfelt connection with your customers.

However, in order to communicate effectively, you need to understand the vehicles of communication. While your messages need to always be consistent, you can't tell your story the same way in an ad as you would on a web site, or in a press release, or through a promotion. Just as you may dress or act differently in different situations, you may need to present your company in different ways to various audiences.

Adapting Your Story

DELIVERY IS HOW you communicate your story and your key messages. The various avenues you use require different ways of telling your story. Here are some of the major types of communication you need to consider.

- investor relations, grant applications
- public relations

- advertising
- customer communications and direct mail
- web site
- trade shows, special events, and promotions
- customer interaction
- employee communications

Through each of these vehicles, you interact with the customer, and he or she gets information about who you are. These points of contact add up to the total experience customers have with you. To ensure their experience is a consistent reflection of who you are, you need to ensure that your personality and spirit are intrinsic to each interaction.

Writing Business Plans and Grant Applications

As we will discuss in the next chapter ("Writing Your Business Plan"), business plans and grant applications require you to concisely tell the story of how your organization will be successful. People use the plan to decide whether to invest in you, and they need to know who you are, as well as learn about your concept, your market, your product or service (or issue), your pricing, your management team. While including stories that succinctly illustrate your commitment and other intangibles can help them get to know you and perhaps even become invested on a more emotional level, the main point is to get the facts out efficiently and effectively to get your story across without wasting any time. You don't want to make the reader work at getting the basic information they need.

Reaching the Public

Public relations is the least glamorous but often most effective way to get your story out to the public. PR is effective because your story is being told by a supposedly objective third party, which gives you a lot more credibility than if you are telling the story yourself. However, it can be limited in terms of reaching the exact, specific audience you want to capture (although this limitation can be alleviated by sending clips of articles or even tape—copies of video or radio coverage of your company or media appearances by your key people to your current and prospective customers). It can also be frustrating because often there is little or no correlation between the magnitude of your PR efforts and how much coverage you actually get.

I always recommend that entrepreneurs who want to do significant public relations work with a PR agency or professional, for many reasons. First, it's terribly easy to get yourself into trouble with PR because you don't have much control over the finished product. If you're not used to working with reporters, you could find yourself in an unfortunate situation before you know it.

Second, you could have quite a learning curve in terms of not only doing PR effectively, but also in terms of researching publications, TV shows, and other avenues. Third, you'll have to cultivate relationships with editors and producers, probably from scratch. PR typically takes a lot of time and effort, and there are many ways for it to go wrong.

If you decide to do your PR yourself, which many people do when they're starting out, here are some basic things to keep in mind.

1. Have a compelling story.

The best way to get PR is to have a good story to tell—one that is of interest to lots of people, not just your mother and competitors. So what is interesting? A new idea or invention . . . A response to or opinion about a hot trend impacting lots of people in new ways . . . Big numbers or dollars . . . And personal stories. In short, stories that are compelling are the ones that get picked up.

Cori Lathan of Anthrotronix has had an unbelievably easy time of getting PR. The media finds her. Why? Because she couldn't have a more compelling story. She works with technology, specifically robots, to help children with disabilities.

A couple of years ago, she was profiled on the evening news because a student in a biomedical engineering college course that she was teaching had invented a hands-free walker, under her supervision. The story featured a darling, precocious, physically challenged child who was enjoying a game of catch with his father for the first time, as Cori and her student looked on. It was a beautiful, touching piece.

They interviewed Cori, her student, the child, and his father. It was such a great story, they ran it twice more the next day during other news shows.

Of course, it didn't hurt that she's a real pro on camera. The piece in question ended on a lighter note, with Cori telling her student, "And by the way—you got an A!" She practically winked at the camera. She had given them the perfect tag to end the story.

A common mistake people make when it comes to public relations is to write the most boring press releases imaginable, including mundane facts and ignoring interesting, human details. You can make anything interesting, if you dig deep enough. (But you still can't make journalists print it, if it doesn't catch their fancy.)

One reason Ella Leya of B-Elite Records was able to garner an amazing amount of publicity to support her newly released CD on her label was that she had such a fascinating personal story to tell. Not only were the songs on her CD about a great loss she endured, but her life has been quite incredible.

Furthermore, her story was rich enough so that each newspaper and radio show could find its own unique angle from which to tell it. One publication, whose readers live on the North Shore of Chicago, focused on the fact that Ella was not your typical rabbi's wife. The *Chicago Tribune Magazine* took readers on a detailed journey of her whole life, documenting the ups and downs and how she survived and transcended her struggles through her love of music. Another publication did an expanded review of the CD, bolstered by details of the loss that inspired her to write it. A radio show segment focused on how she adapted to the United States and got noticed in the music business. Yet another focused on the various, eclectic influences in her music. Her story had something for everyone, and she did her research to find out what each publication or show might be interested in and adapted her media kit and cover letter to fit their needs.

2. Tell your story clearly.

Who, what, when, where, why. That's the basis for a press release. Press releases follow a specific form. You need to follow that form, and make sure that all the basics are there. You can always back up the press release with further material, but don't make editors work to find the information, because they probably won't.

If you can include professional photos, you increase your chances of getting picked up. Provide quotes from key people where you can. If you can provide customer testimonials or case studies, so much the better. Always give contact information, including the name and direct telephone number. For employment press releases (promotions, new hires, etc.), include the person's age; for some reason, your chances of being picked up are often better if you do so, although this appears to be changing.

When you first make contact with a publication, you should send them a media kit including not only the press release announcing the launch of your company (or some other relevant event or milestone, if your company has been in existence for a while), but also some or all of the following:

- company profile
- company history
- management team bios (and photos, if available—and professional)
- product or service information
- capabilities brochure or other material
- your business card
- case studies
- reprints of past articles

You should introduce yourself with a friendly cover letter, and it never hurts to follow up with a phone call.

One final note: check everything for typos. Your PR material should be as close to perfect as possible.

3. Find the appropriate publications and adapt your stories.

You need to think through which audiences you are trying to reach with your public relations efforts. Who are your ideal customers or investors? You then need to determine how they get information. What publications do they read? What shows do they watch?

You can try to ensure that you are telling your story in a way that will interest specific publications. You can request circulation and editorial information from most publications. Many magazines or journals have editorial calendars for the entire year including their features and focuses. They will often tell you how and when to submit topics for articles (or even written articles, especially for trade publications), topics covered by various editors, and other relevant information.

When that information is not available, you can improve your chances of getting your story picked up by reading the publication, especially the work by writers and editors who cover your type of information. What types of stories do they write? What is their style? What type of angle do they take? And . . . do you know anyone who knows them? Do you know anyone who knows anyone who knows them? After all, in many cases, it's still a relationship game. (That's one of the primary values of using a PR firm—their established relationships.)

4. Run everything by a lawyer (but be prepared to fight back).

It pains me to say it, but there it is. You can open yourself up to great risk when you put information out into the world. You want to shout out your story from the rooftops, but PR requires you to be careful. Then again, lawyers are paid to be paranoid. You're probably going to have to make some judgment calls to find the sweet spot between those two perspectives.

Here's the straight scoop. PR people and lawyers share a purpose—to protect the company. They have to work together closely, especially in sensitive times, such as during a crisis, an acquisition, or financial reporting. However, they often find themselves at odds because they "protect the company" in very different ways. Some of the best fights I have ever witnessed or in which I have taken part have been between the communicators and the lawyers.

This is how it usually unfolds, at least in bigger companies. The communicator writes the press release, as concisely and clearly as possible. Then the simple document, which is usually only three or four short paragraphs long, makes its way through a lengthy and painful approval process. At some point (or at many points) in that process, the lawyers get their hands on it. Often lawyers are frustrated writers. Often they are talented writers, as well—but they've been trained to do legal writing, which is quite a different animal than what most professional communicators do. The result of the lawyers' handiwork is sometimes an incomprehensible, passively worded, frightening document that sounds as if the company is paranoid, defensive, or guilty of major crimes. Often, they have rewritten various aspects of the document that have absolutely no legal bearing (remember, they are frustrated writers).

This is where the fight begins. The key is to determine which changes are legally relevant, and then to ignore or fight their other changes until you have a document that clearly provides your information while not opening yourself up to any legal risks. This whole scenario plays itself out repeatedly throughout corporate communications departments the world over.

5. Be prepared.

Reporters may call you back to ask questions about your press release or media kit. They may also call you for other reasons, which may entail talking about things you don't want to share. You have to be prepared to handle any circumstance. This is why it is advisable to get training to deal with crises, rumors, questions you don't want to or legally can't answer, or hire someone else to manage it.

Some thoughts on "no comment." You want to avoid the "no comment" in most cases. You can have other statements at the ready, including the good old standby's, such as variations on the following: "We do not discuss industry rumors," "We do not share confidential details of an ongoing investigation," or "Our first concern is for the safety of our employees." They qualify as an answer, whereas "no comment" looks like you're hiding something.

I was always taught to "never say 'no comment.'" I believed it. Then, a few years ago, a minor but arrogant rock band decided to stir up some publicity by adapting a version of John Lennon's famously misunderstood comment that the Beatles were bigger than Jesus by saying that their own mildly successful band was "bigger than God." It was a blatant attempt to get attention, and it worked. The newspapers reported it, and then also reported that the spokesperson for one global religion responded by saying something like, "Well, they've only been around for a few years, and God's been around for a lot longer than that." They actually were defending God! If ever there were a time for "no comment," that was it. It was the exception that proves the rule. Other than that, it's good to have another response at the ready.

It Pays to Advertise—Sometimes.

WHILE ADVERTISING IS the most glamorous of the ways you can get your story out, it often won't get you new clients so much as bolster or reinforce your messages, brand and identity. You can control your advertising messages, which is a pro, but you lack the credibility of having a third party discuss who you are, which is a con. Obviously, it's your ad so you're going to say good things about yourself.

There are three basic kinds of advertising. One is image advertising, the goal of which is to establish your corporate or brand identity, and to heighten overall good feeling about your company, product or service, like Nike's "Just do it" ads. The second is direct response advertising, which aims to generate business or sell products. This often includes a "call to action" 800 number or web site for "trackability." Many phone carrier ads, for example, do this kind of advertising. A third kind is benefit-focused advertising. These ads highlight a key benefit (or two or three, but that's harder and arguably less effective), such as Timex's "takes a licking but keeps on ticking" ads.

Advertising can be extremely effective at supporting your brand or identity. It may be less effective at selling your products, although that depends on whether you are using the right kind of advertising. People often overestimate the importance and effect of advertising when it comes to selling products, and then are disappointed that they don't see an immediate upturn in sales. In many cases, my advice for a new business—although it obviously depends on your specific situation—is to take it easy on the advertising dollars in the beginning, and focus more on PR and direct mail.

Another piece of advertising advice: beware the retainer payment setup! Advertising dollars can quickly spiral out of control. Also, be sure your advertising people will work well with (i.e., respect the ideas of) your PR people. And beware the agencies that jump to creative, instead of working through strategy—by which

I mean they start throwing out ideas for commercials without laying out first what they hope to achieve in business terms and how.

How to Choose a PR Firm

WHEN HIRING A PR agency or professional, here are some things to consider.

- ALWAYS LOOK AT SEVERAL DIFFERENT AGENCIES OF DIFFERENT SIZES.

  It's a good idea to interview several agencies or individuals, bring in at least three of the ones you are most comfortable with, learn about them, and have them bid on your project. You can learn a great deal from initial presentations from different firms, not only about what services they provide and what they specialize in, but also about what they're like as people and how they interact. It's also useful to tell them what your basic goals are and to ask their take on how you can use PR to achieve some of your goals. You can become an informed consumer just by listening closely to different agencies' ideas for your firm. I've also found that in most cases several different agencies can meet a client's basic needs, so the final decision is often made by instinct and comfort level.

- MAKE SURE THEY HAVE RESOURCES AND RELATIONSHIPS, IN ADDITION TO THE BASIC SKILLS.

  A professional may have the skills to do the job, but not the resources in terms of people and access to information or relationships with the right people in the media. Find out who they know and how they get things done. Ask who their clients are, and call them, not just the specific references you're given. If you choose a big agency, make sure up front that you will not be lost in the shuffle of bigger clients. And make sure you meet the team of people who will be working with you on a daily basis.

BE CLEAR ABOUT THE DELIVERABLES YOU WANT, AND KNOW WHAT YOU ARE PAYING FOR.

In the beginning, you may want an industry analysis; the creation of a media list of publications, shows, etc., you'd like to target; development of strategic messages; and creation of basic material, including media kits and press releases (discussed below). You may also want to have them create media guidelines, including policies and examples of standard press releases for various situations, such as:

- employment releases
- acquisitions
- major deals
- new products or services
- financial information
- customer successes.

And finally, you may want media training for key people, as well as the development of a crisis communication plan.

BE VERY CAREFUL ABOUT PAYMENT TERMS.

Agencies and professionals on their own often ask for monthly retainers, for a year or two. While this has been standard in the past, I highly recommend avoiding the retainer setup until the agency or individuals have proven themselves. If you do enter into some sort of retainer, be sure you have the right to cancel anytime, with thirty days notice, or include some other out in the contract in case you're not happy. But remember, PR takes time. You can't expect overnight results in terms of coverage, especially if you don't have a good story.

AND FINALLY, LOOK FOR STRATEGY!

Some PR agencies tend to be tactical instead of strategic. By that I mean that they jump to tactics—for example, offering a plan with a laundry list of projects without specifying overall strategic objectives, such as writing a bunch of press

releases and try to get some mentions in the papers. An example of a strategic objective is the following: to establish the company's people as industry experts to attract the clients we want (who value expertise above all). That objective will be achieved by doing the laundry list—writing opinion pieces and working with editors to get key people interviewed on industry trends by the best trade papers, for example—but the list of tactics is within the context of strategy. You'll know the difference right off if they jump to tactics without trying to learn about your objectives, your competitors, and your industry.

Reaching Your Customer Directly

WITH CUSTOMER COMMUNICATIONS and direct mail, the key is to be able to put yourself in their shoes and address what matters to them, instead of what you want them to hear. What keeps them up at night? What do they need the most? What is the value you bring to them? Why should they care? Why should they open your mail? You can convey information about who you are along the way, but your main focus should be answering their major questions. To do this, you have to figure out who your ideal target customers are, and then find out what's important to them. Research is always helpful to learn what they most care about, and to determine how what you do intersects with what they need.

Then, of course, you need to be able to reach them. You need to keep track of your existing customers, and you need to find ways to reach prospective customers. You can do this in a variety of ways:

1. You can buy lists of target customers from trade publications, industry associations, or list distributors.
2. You can find existing distribution channels.

One established but small theater company wanted to attract younger professionals in a certain geographic area, yet they had almost no budget. They couldn't afford to buy lists or pay for a huge direct mailing. Instead, they partnered with some groups and associations whose members fit their profile, including local chapters of alumni clubs, singles groups, professionals groups, as well as a local "social club" that sponsored athletic events and huge parties for its thousands of members in that area. By offering discount nights for the club's membership, or jointly sponsoring a benefit or promotion, for example, they reached the population they wanted and raised their profile, using the other groups' mailing lists and resources.

If you can't create it, partner with someone who already has it, or something close to it.

Breaking Through the Clutter

THE KEY TO effective direct mail is to break through the clutter. People get lots of junk mail. The goal is to create something memorable that is impossible to throw away. You can do that with a great offer, a cool design, a funny headline . . . in short, a piece with a little extra magic or personality to it.

You get junk mail every day, right? Consider what works for you, what keeps you interested enough in a piece that you get that you actually hold on to it. Your direct mail should never be a throwaway. Instead, it can be a piece of art that expresses who you are.

Making the Most of Every Communications Piece

PERSONALITY CAN BE expressed in even the most basic pieces. Joe Bardetti, a world-class freelance copywriter, actor, playwright and stand-up comedian, showcases his sense of humor and personality in his business cards and resume. His two-sided business cards come in several colors, each with one side featuring a picture of his friendly face (the same picture that winks at you from his web site, www.bardetti.com). Above the picture is one of several different funny statements, such as "The bigger the hair, the closer to God," and "Real Italian comedy just like Mama used to make." On the other side is his information, including his web site e-mail address, followed by the statement, "Come on over and give me a cyber-squeeze."

Joe's resume, which he uses for copywriting work, includes sections entitled, "Clients, Friends and Drinkin' Buddies," "Bowling Trophies and Other Awards," and "Hobbies and Obsessions." Another section, called "My Creative Work Turns Up in the Darndest Places," lists "television," "print," "radio," and "soggy bar napkins." His objective? "To obtain work as a freelance copywriter and/or rocket scientist." This one-page document not only informs the reader of Joe's stellar education, impressive client roster, and prestigious awards, but it also gives you a taste of his personality. You know exactly what you're getting when you hire him.

So you see? No piece of marketing material is too small to effectively communicate who you are.

Catching the Wave

WHEN IT COMES to surfing the web, people don't like to read. They don't like to have to search too hard for things. And they don't like to wait.

Copy on web sites need to be personal, entertaining, conversational, and—above all—concise! Boring won't cut it—people will be gone with a click. And nothing is more boring than staring at a blank screen while something loads. Simple is better. Don't frustrate your customers with bells and whistles, unless that best serves your product or service, or your customer base is impressed by—and certain to have—the latest, fastest, best technology.

Use short bites of copy—concise, clear sentences, in bullet form where possible. Make sure the site is constructed in a logical way, and that nothing is more than two clicks away. A search function is good to have, if you can afford it.

Funny is good. Irreverent is often OK, depending on your clients and who you are. Showing personality (authentic, of course) on your web site is crucial. (In fact, I've noticed that this kind of web site writing is having an impact on corporate writing in general. Companies who used to not only settle for, but actually prefer dry writing are now searching for entertaining copy in short bites.)

Make sure your site is designed and supported well. If your site is down or difficult to use, you'll lose people. If it makes sense for you and your business, and if you can afford it, you can always provide a personal, interactive touch on your site by making good use of the technology. Automatic responses, such as "thank you's" or "we received your order/comments and will get back to you within 24 hours," add a nice, personal touch. Of course, you have to do what you promise, or you'll lose credibility.

I've dealt with numerous web site development companies. There are tons of them, although not as many as there used to be, and they usually come from one of three backgrounds: techie, creative, or strategic. Techie people often come from technical backgrounds and focus on the technology first and foremost, whereas creatives (who usually come from ad agency or design backgrounds) care most about the look and feel, tone and style of the web site. Strategic people tend to come from marketing or general business backgrounds, and they are most concerned about developing a site that will help you meet your business objectives.

You'll usually find companies strong in one of these areas; you'll sometimes find a company strong in two areas; and I have yet to find a company strong in all three (within a reasonable budget, anyway). Do you need a highly technical e-business site? Or do you just need a site that is basically an online brochure that looks cool? If you come across someone who starts by asking you about your marketing objectives, get excited. But be clear about what they can do and what you really need.

I had one client who hired a company run by brilliant marketing guys who created a great web strategy and a useful site map, but whose designs were shockingly bad. Turns out the "designer" was an MBA who liked to play with the computer. We cut our losses, kept the site map, and worked with a company of former advertising creatives who had gone into the web site development world. They would not necessarily have been very helpful in terms of developing a strategy, but they came up with a gorgeous look.

Putting On Great Special Events and Promotions

PEOPLE OFTEN DON'T realize that their promotions and special events can be a strategic way to get business and to communicate their key messages. A successful event or promotion is defined not only by the attendance or the level of response you've achieved but also by what your customer learns about who you are and what you do.

The most effective promotions and events are those that not only engage the customer in a way that meets your specific objective but also communicate who you are and the value that you provide. For example, one client recently did an extremely effective promotion to try to get its salespeople in the door of several hundred potential clients. This company, a technology company that is breaking into the consulting arena, provides a great value to clients in that they can not only make high level recommendations but they can also build the systems and make them work, unlike many consulting firms. To get across the point of their mentality— "We can build it too!"—they offered high-quality workboots to clients who answered the promotion (delivered in person by the salesperson, of course). They received a response rate well above the typical good response rate for a promotion (usually around 3 to 10 percent). This was a successful promotion because the company not only got in the doors of potential clients (conversion rates to real business are still being tracked), but also because they communicated a key value and a major part of their identity.

Similarly, special events can be a powerful way to connect with customers. A special event can be unique. A meeting or a conference can truly be taken to a whole new level—the level of an experience. We've all been to meetings and conferences; we know how they usually go. In planning events, you can work against people's expectations. You can surprise and delight them with an unexpected visitor or performance. . . . You can teach them something or inspire them with an out-of-sight motivational speaker. . . . You can give them an opportunity to experience your company in a new way with unusual, fun, team-building activities or creative challenges with your employees. It doesn't have to cost more money (although it can). It just takes a little bit of inspiration, that extra effort to make it something special.

It's in the details. Say you're unveiling a new program, and you hope to add excitement and emphasize to employees that they are the true stars of the show. Why not present it like a movie premiere and hold it at a famous theater instead of the typical hotel ballroom? What about adding a red carpet for the employees, and paparazzi at the door, yelling and flashing lightbulbs to create excitement? How about movie star lookalikes? Invitations in the form of backstage passes? Old time popcorn machines? That's what an ad agency did recently to introduce its new vision. The high-energy feel and variation from the usual meeting sent a strong message that this was different—not just another new initiative—and something to celebrate.

Here's how I look at it: if you're going to do it, do it right. Create an adventure, and take people for a ride. But do it in a way that also helps you achieve your specific strategic objective.

Interacting with Customers

Every interaction you have with your customer—including their experience with your product—builds your brand or identity. From your product to the experience they have when they work with any of your people or order from your web site . . . it all tells them who you are. The whole experience informs them.

It is important to think through every single point at which you touch your customers throughout their entire relationship with you, and to determine how you want to express who you are through each interaction. One way to consistently express your personality is to write prototype letters and scripts for every customer interaction throughout the process, from the first contact to the sale through customer service, to ensure uniformity of messages. You and your people may choose to only rarely follow the exact script or prototype letter in every case, but it gives everyone a sense of how to deal with your customer in a way that best represents your company.

Word of mouth is a crucial form of marketing. Your customers can be your most important and effective marketers. You can't control word of mouth—all you can do is try to ensure the highest quality experience for your customers. Loyal customers can bring you a great deal of business.

I was recently reminded of this when I bought an artistic, interesting shirt. Every time I wore it, people commented on how unique it was. It was like wearing a piece of art!

A few weeks later, I came across two more shirts in the same style, made by the same company. I bought them too. My friends started getting jealous of my new look! I became known as "the woman with all the cool shirts" by several people at a company with which I had just begun to consult. I felt like a walking billboard for this product!

I searched the Internet for this company, and hit on its web site the very first day it was up and running. Obviously, I ordered more shirts (including one for my sister, which I kept). I also called my most vociferously jealous friend and told her about the web site. Ten minutes later, she had ordered three shirts. We made a secret pact not to tell anyone else our secret.

Of course, being me, I've broken this pact repeatedly and told everyone I know about this site. Now, it seems almost every time I go out wearing one of my cool shirts, at least one person I'm with is wearing a similar one. (Also being me, I had to check out the messages on the web site. I was not surprised to see that they had included their mission as a company, which included "inspiring" others with their products. You can see and feel that passion in their T-shirts.)

Sometimes, if customers are happy enough, they will actively recruit new business for you. I was so blown away by the independent film *Hedwig and the Angry Inch* that I not only told lots of people about it (including sending a mass e-mail), but I also actively convinced many to see it, going so far as to drag (so to speak) numerous friends to the theater, on several different occasions. Many of them may never have heard about the film, or if they had, would probably not have gone to see it. Now I have lots of happy friends who have experienced it—and they are telling lots of their friends, and so on, and so on. A simple chain reaction like that can translate into meaningful business—and in fact many smaller film production companies and studios count on this word of mouth for survival.

Helping Employees Communicate Through Sales Support

YOUR PEOPLE ARE major marketers of your company. In order to express who you are as a company, they have to fully understand it and be prepared to communicate it through their words and actions.

You can never communicate too much with your people. You have to continually express and reinforce your messages through words and actions. You also need to give employees the training and materials they need to market the company effectively. Basically, this means providing varying levels of sales support for all of the people in your company.

If you are hiring a sales force, you should develop a basic customer presentation, talking points, or scripts to describe the company and its product offering, and some form of training. Most companies do this to some extent. What many neglect to do is recognize that employees throughout the company need some level of training and sales support as well to effectively market your company.

Here are some basic tips for keeping employees prepared and informed:

1. Provide every employee with training and written materials capturing your identity, including your vision, mission, values and key messages.
2. Continually reinforce those messages.

   Restate the messages over and over, in written and verbal communications with your people. Communicate within the framework of the key messages. Tell stories that illustrate and exemplify the key messages.
3. Keep employees informed of customer communications.

   Always inform employees of any communications with customers, including direct mail campaigns or promotions, new advertisements, an update to your web site, or the release of a new press release. Anytime you release any communication to the media, industry, or your customers, you should provide employees with a copy of what you're releasing, an explanation of the strategy behind it, and even talking points to answer any questions about it. This not only supports your efforts, but it emphasizes the important role each employee plays in expressing who you are to the world.
4. Solicit input and feedback to ensure employee support.

   If they don't agree with your key messages or responses, employees will not support—and in some cases may even undercut—your story. Their enlistment is necessary, and the information they provide can be helpful in ensuring your communications is the best it can be and is consistent with what the customers are experiencing and feeling.

Can any of these forms of communications help you achieve your specific marketing objectives?

How can PR help you achieve your objectives? Can you think of any compelling stories you have to tell about your company, concept, or product that might be of interest to the general or trade media. Are you doing anything new, different, or first? Are there any interesting human interest angles to your story?

Can advertising help you achieve any of your objectives? What is the major value of your product or service that you would like to communicate?

Imagine the ultimate promotion for your company that effectively expresses your company's identity.

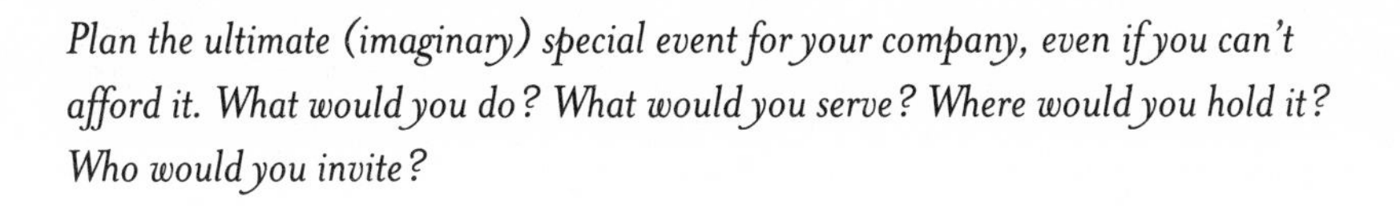

Plan the ultimate (imaginary) special event for your company, even if you can't afford it. What would you do? What would you serve? Where would you hold it? Who would you invite?

Imagine your customer's interactions with your company. Write out the ideal experience you'd like a customer to have, from when they first hear of you until their interaction is complete.

In the next chapter, we will address how to write your marketing plan and marketing communications plan.

Nine

REACHING YOUR GOALS

9. develop concrete goals and flexible strategies

HERE'S ONE THING I know: things change. Sometimes, they change really quickly. So, while it's crucial to set forth and commit to concrete goals, it's important to recognize that your strategies for getting there may have to change with the environment around you. Sure, sometimes your goals will change too, and that's OK—but your strategies are just paths to your destination and require extreme flexibility. If a big boulder falls in front of the path you're on, you need to jump out of the way and find—or create—another route.

The most successful, effective businesses I've seen are those who can say, "OK, we tried that and it's not working well enough, so now we're going to try this," and then make the leap to the new way quickly and completely, without losing sight of their ultimate goals. It's not a sign of failure; it's just life. We can't predict everything, we can just do our best to look ahead and then adapt, hopefully quickly, to whatever life has in store.

Changing your strategy can take a great deal of courage. I once worked for a division of a company that had invested millions of dollars creating a new service, based on groundbreaking software, for an industry they had never before served. To serve this industry, the company had to prepare for huge public safety issues, building foolproof, redundant safety mechanisms into their systems and processes. Years' worth of research was done to create the service. The company had also determined the potential implications and cost of a catastrophe, and it was decided by the parent company that the risk was acceptable, given the extreme focus on safety in creating the new service.

Then, suddenly, the climate changed. An accident occurred to a competitor, and the results were different than expected, in terms of its scope and implications. Literally the day before the company was to sign its first multiyear deal, the parent company pulled the plug. Years of work, millions of dollars, several people's jobs were involved—yet the CEO of the parent company made a quick decision, just before the new division was about to go past the point of no return. The division was shut down, and it was sad, but the decision was a strong, valid one in light of the changed risk-reward equation.

Another client of mine has been in the health care industry for over twenty years. As regulatory changes have occurred, she's changed the services and the focus of her company several times to protect her company, her people, and her clients' best interests. She has stayed true to her mission of serving the community with her services, but the way she has done it—the specific types of services—has changed based on the regulatory environment.

Your Life

Setting Goals is Easy . . .

. . . IT'S THE GETTING there part that's hard. And part of getting there is having a plan.

The New Year's Resolution is the perfect case in point. At the beginning of every year, we often set for ourselves ambitious goals, but we don't give much thought to how we are—realistically—going to achieve them.

One year, a friend of mine decided she was going to run a marathon. It was the middle of the winter, and the marathon wasn't until the following October, so she bought a book on how to train and then pretty much forgot about it during the long winter. Then, life got in the way and before she knew it, it was mid-July. She pulled out the book, and then realized she was already supposed to be doing long runs of more than ten miles! She got right out there, did a long run, and pulled a hamstring.

The following year, she decided she'd give it another shot. She recruited some friends to run with her and joined a running group for the long runs. She started training in earnest, running with her friend during the week and with the group on the long runs on Sunday morning, along the lakefront. Then, her friends dropped out . . . and, as the summer wore on and the runs got longer, the group began meeting earlier and earlier to beat the heat. One Sunday, her alarm went off at 4:30 A.M., and she faced the prospect of running sixteen miles in the heat at five in the morning . . . and she rolled over and happily, if guiltily, went back to sleep. From that point on, she ran when she could, missing some shorter runs, and then pulling a calf muscle on a long run because she wasn't prepared. She dropped out.

Another year passed. This year, she got serious. She has a real plan and strategies.

- ✦ STRATEGY 1: Prepare and stick to a schedule. She has recorded every short and long run during her training period on her calendar, which is prominently displayed where she can't help but see it. She has circled each long run, and counts them each as a minor goal (and victory, when she finishes them) on the way to her ultimate goal. She's made most of the runs so far.

- ✦ STRATEGY 2: Have a lot of support and more than one partner. In case one or more of her running partners drops out or gets injured, she has three different running partners. One of them is usually available to run with her, or to keep her motivated when she is tired or wants to give up.
- ✦ STRATEGY 3: Be prepared. This year, she is doing everything she can not to get injured. She has the right shoes, the right stuff (gel to eat, heart rate watch, sports drinks, high-tech fabric running clothes). She is icing, she is stretching, she is cross-training. She's ready.

So, I'm happy to report, she's on track (so to speak) to achieve her goal of running a marathon. She knows herself and what she needs to work through her weaknesses, and she has learned from past failures and developed strategies to work past them. Whereas in the past she was approaching her goal in a somewhat unplanned, undisciplined way, this year she is doing the necessary planning and work to actually run that marathon.

The point is, have a goal, but then break it down into ways you can get there successfully. Whatever your personal goals—get in shape, find new office space, learn how to hang glide—the chances of you achieving it are greatly increased if you carve out a plan and a path for yourself. Small steps lead to great journeys!

Set one or more personal goals for yourself that you'd really like to reach but have had trouble achieving. Then, develop at least three strategies for how you will reach your goal. Make sure you create your strategies that you can successfully follow. Then, set up a reasonable schedule with some smaller goals along the way. Make sure your first goal, especially, seems easily achieved, and that each goal leading up to your final goal is not too great a leap to achieve. If your strategies don't work, then change them using what you've learned.

Your Company

Planning to Achieve Your Vision

PLANS ARE JUST tools to get where you want to go. If you have a vision, you already know where that is. Now, you have to develop the road map to get there.

Business seems filled with plans. Business plans. Financial plans. Marketing plans. Communications plans. Account management plans. Employee relations plans. You can dress them up with graphics, stuff them with numbers, decorate them with pie charts, whatever. They're still just road maps. Not scary, just road maps.

Simple plans are better than complicated ones, and not just because our eyes don't glaze over when we read them. Simple plans are easy to explain. They're easy to understand. They're easy to believe in. They're easy to get behind.

That doesn't mean they don't require thought, energy, and research. It just means they make sense and are clearly communicated.

I always start at the highest level and then work my way down to the details. I start with who we want to be and what we do. Every plan we create should help us stick to our knitting and reach our ultimate goals. Every plan I write, whether it's a marketing plan or an employee relations plan, starts with the company vision and mission. That keeps us grounded.

There are several types of plans that you may need to create. The scope, size or complexity of your business will dictate what your actual plan will need to be like, and these brief explanations can hardly cover everything you'd need to know to create full-blown plans, but I will include brief descriptions of several of these types of plans. I will also lay out for you my simple approach for creating the types of plans you may need. With this approach, your plans flow logically from your ultimate goals and so all work together to get you where you want to be. While this approach may not fit every company's needs, it is at least one way to think about planning.

Creating Your Corporate Identity Plan

THE FIRST PLAN I help create for a new company is not the business plan, as you might suspect, but the corporate identity plan. Here's what it entails:

- Your vision
- Your mission
- Your key values
- Your profile
- Your key messages (including features and benefits)
- Your high level strategies

This is your original, source document. It is an internal document, that is, one that will not be shared with clients in this format. This is a great document to give to every employee, new and existing, as well as to any agencies or consultants who may work with you. It is basically a statement of who you are and/or who you hope to be.

Happily, if you've done the exercises in this book, you've already created all of these aspects except for your high-level strategies. Let's do that now.

Your high level strategies are the ways you plan to achieve your vision. It is how you are going to get from here to there. For example, if your goal is to be the top corporate and commercial video producer in the tristate area, your high-level strategies might be as follows:

1. Start by becoming respected niche player in artistic, stylized video, attracting premium price
2. Recruit and retain the most talented creatives in the area
3. Purchase the best equipment available
4. Identify and pursue only clients who are interested in doing artistic, stylized work and attract them with excellent personal service and exciting creative
5. Open an office in this city initially, and then open branches in three other major cities in the tristate area

6. Identify and acquire small production houses in the state who do top-quality work of this type
7. Identify and partner with ad agencies who use production companies to do top-quality work of this type

Your strategies, then, should answer the questions, "How will you grow?" and "How will you achieve your vision?" These strategies complete your corporate identity, and serve as the basis for all of your other plans.

Develop your high-level strategies for inclusion in your corporate identity plan. Try to cover all the important elements of how you will achieve your vision, but keep it general. Usually, five to seven strategy statements will suffice.

Writing Your Business Plan

BUSINESS PLANS USUALLY are created to do one of two things: to get funding or to serve as a reminder to stick to your knitting. They should be concise, not more than fifteen pages.

While there are millions of ways to write a business plan (and hundreds of books to tell you how to do it or consultants who can help you), here are the basic elements your business plan should discuss:

1. YOUR IDEA

This is where you tell your company's story to potential investors and make your case for its economic viability and growth potential. In other words, you answer the question, why should anyone invest in this company? In this section, you discuss:

Your Products or Services

- What's your big idea? What products or services do you offer? How are they unique? How are they different and better than what's already out there? If nothing else is out there, why is that?
- Discuss the market, including clients, competitors, and the industry. You need to include market research to describe your competitors and industry to answer these questions: Who are the competitors? How big are they? Who are their customers? How do they operate? How do you plan to impact these competitors? What is the size of the industry? What challenges does it face? What need are you filling or creating? Who are your potential customers?

You can hire a consultant or market research firm to help you, or you can do the research yourself, using the Internet, consulting industry magazines and trade journals, buying information from companies that sell lists or industry/company reports, or signing up with an online research service like Lexis-Nexis.

Your Pricing

- How much will your products or services cost? How did you arrive at that number? Do they cost more or less than those of your competitors? Why?

Promotion

- How will you get the word out? You don't have to get into details here. You can stay at a high level, hitting on your overall strategy for marketing your company. For example, the video company might decide to use a direct sales force and a targeted direct mail marketing campaign to get clients, and they may also choose to partner with existing production houses, backed up by moderate advertising in trade magazines. That is the level of detail we're discussing at this point.

Developing your idea in this section is a great test for whether or not the idea is a business. Through the research, you can test the idea. You need to validate, revalidate, and then validate again. Build your case, but be conservative with your numbers; it's better to under-promise and over-deliver than the alternative. Besides, your goal is to build a successful business, not drum up money for a business that can't succeed.

Let's say you're doing something that is new to the industry. If there's not an example of the type of service you plan to provide within your industry, you can always use another example in a different industry that could be analogous to your situation. If you have difficulty making your case, you can be creative in trying to persuade potential investors of the validity of your idea.

2. You

Here's where you tell potential investors why you're more worthy of their money than anyone else—not just direct competitors, but any other entrepreneurs or companies that may want their money, because at this point, that's who you're competing with. Why are you (and your people) the right person (or people) to run this company? What are your skills, experience, background, education, talents that make you the best person for them to bet on? You don't need to include the amount of detail that would be in a resume; a paragraph or two that encapsulate your abilities and experience should suffice.

3. Financials

You should know your costs inside and out. That includes staffing costs, manufacturing costs, operations costs, and promotions costs. How much money will you need? When will you start making money? How much, how soon? You should include your profit and loss estimates — how much you will spend and how much you will make each year for at least the next three years, but preferably up to five years out.

In terms of the level of detail, you can keep it high level. For example, for staffing costs, you could include the number of people, their basic functions, and the total costs for them, for each year. For promotion costs, you could list "Advertising, Trade Shows, Direct Mail," and then the cost for each year. You can include the details in an appendix, if you choose, and you should know your reasoning behind each of the costs, but you do not need to bowl the potential investors over with details.

Begin a draft of the business plan, filling in what you can. Make a note of where you need to do research to fill out the rest of the sections.

Developing Your Marketing Plan

YOUR MARKETING PLAN includes anything that has to do with attracting and keeping clients, positioning your company in the eyes of the outside world, or doing market research. A typical marketing plan will include the following elements:

- Target customers
- Customer segmentation
- Buy scenarios
- Channels you use to go to market
- Partnerships and strategic relationships
- Positioning
- Promotion
- Metrics

Again, there are millions of ways to do marketing plans, and I will not profess to teach you how to do a full and complete marketing plan in a couple of pages, so instead I will lay out a general approach to creating one that fits into your overall goals. To do your actual plan, you may want to work with a consultant or use one of the many books out there that will explain in full the more complicated aspects of marketing.

As always, your marketing plan should start out with your vision and your ultimate goals. You can also include your high-level strategy points that deal directly with marketing. Using our example above, that is:

Vision: to be the top video producer of high-quality, artistic, stylized video in the tristate area

High-level strategies:

- ✦ Start by becoming a respected niche player in artistic, stylized video, attracting premium price
- ✦ Identify and pursue only clients who are interested in doing artistic, stylized work and attract them with excellent personal service and exciting creative
- ✦ Identify and partner with ad agencies who use production companies to do top-quality work of this type

Now, the question becomes, how can we use the various areas of marketing—including marketing communications, market research, and direct sales—to do this? We have to break it down. Let's use one of the high-level strategies here and look at how we will address it within the marketing plan.

1. Start by becoming a respected niche player in artistic, stylized video, attracting premium price.

Product/Service

So, the strategy to become an artistic video producer in the tristate area is to first develop a reputation as a respected producer of the best, most expensive type of video.

First, we need to figure out what it means to achieve this in terms of our products and services. What is the market for this type of video in the tristate area? Who are the leading players now? We need to gather a great deal of information, and make informed estimations if we can't find actual dollars. Then we need to set goals for our company. How much business do we want to do each year until we achieve our goal? How much should we charge? How many clients a year do we need? How much revenue? These decisions are somewhat arbitrary, but we need a basic plan we can work toward.

We can always change going forward. Say we plan in the first year to find ten clients who each spend between $50k and $75k, but we only come up with three clients, but one spends $400k and the other two spend $200k between them. We may want to change our approach to focus on finding fewer clients with bigger budgets and retaining them; or we may decide we need more clients for the sake of diversifying in a volatile marketplace in case we lose one of our big clients. You have to do the research and then make the judgment calls.

Next, we need to determine how the other elements of marketing will help us achieve this goal.

Marketing Communications

We can use marketing communications to help position ourselves as a great new choice for artistic, stylized video. Let's say we want to do moderate PR to develop credibility and let people know who we are and advertising to entice people to use us by focusing on a unique benefit we offer in local advertising trade papers. We also want to do a targeted direct mail campaign to companies who do this kind of video. We'd need to include a goal for each area of marketing communications we plan to use, as well as a dollar figure for how much money we need. (We'll go into more detail in the marketing communications plan.)

Direct Sales

Say we also want to use direct sales to drum up clients. What are our goals and objectives for the salesperson or sales force? How many sales people will we need? How much will each sale cost? How will we structure the compensation plan? How much revenue or how many clients will they sign up?

Create an initial draft of your marketing plan, filling in what you can and making note of what you need to do to fill in the gaps.

Developing Your Marketing Communications Plan

AS WITH YOUR marketing plan, your marketing communications plan should begin with the ultimate goal of achieving you company's vision, and should unfold from there, including your strategies and objectives. Your marketing communications plan should support these objectives, and should include the tactics you will use to achieve them.

If you do not have a communications background, you will undoubtedly find it useful to work with a professional to flesh this plan out, but in the meantime, this will be a useful way to start thinking about your plan.

Let's continue on with our example from above to see how the marketing communications plan flows out from the marketing plan and corporate identity.

Vision: to be the top video producer of high-quality, artistic, stylized video in the tri-state area

High level strategy: Start by becoming a respected niche player in artistic, stylized video, attracting premium price

Next, we'll want to capture our objective for marketing communications, in light of this high-level strategy. So how about this:

Objective: to use marketing communications to introduce our company to the industry and position it as a top-quality video producer of artistic stylized video because we have the most creative people, and to attract new clients.

OK, before we lay out our tactics, we have to develop our creative strategy and our media strategy (defined below).

The creative strategy is how we want to sell ourselves. Who are our target customers and what do they value? What is the benefit we offer to them? How do we communicate that?

In our example, say our target clients are people who do artistic, stylized video, who care about quality and who are willing and able to pay top dollar. Let's say, in our research, we've discovered that these clients are companies who make or market high-end luxury products. We have a list of these clients, and we've talked to a few of them, and they've told us that what they want more than anything is really groundbreaking, original work that creates a buzz around their product. Part of our strategy is to hire the very best in the field, the most talented filmmakers out there, who come up with the most creative videos and films. So that's what we're going to sell. When you work with us, you get the most creative videos out there that generates excitement around your product. You get works of genius that generate buzz.

Now, if we want to position ourselves as creative geniuses, we need to express that in the way we write and present ourselves. The copy, the graphics, the tone, should all say "creative genius!" But let's say we know our clients want to work with friendly, fun creative geniuses, as opposed to cold, irrational ones. They are sick of working with creatives who are difficult and unapproachable. In fact, they're frustrated creatives themselves, and they want to be involved in the project. We decide to use that, and we back it up with the fact that our people are the best and our approach to customer service is collaborative. We reflect that in our tone as well, even in our slogan and selling proposition: "Share the buzz!"

You get the point. Your advertising agency, if you choose to work with one, or your own internal marketing people can help you develop this, but here you go for now. So our plan should say something like:

Creative Strategy:

Sell to makers and marketers (ad agencies) of high-end, luxury products

Position as collaborative, creative geniuses that create groundbreaking, original videos that create buzz around products

- Our people are the most creative in the industry!
- Our process and approach is to collaborate with our clients every step of the way

"Share the buzz!"

Next, we need to develop our media strategy, which simply means where we are going to advertise. Our goal is to reach as many of the right people as directly and inexpensively as possible. So, you have to find out what your target clients read.

In our example, we determine from our research that our target clients read certain advertising trade publications. It is expensive to pay for ads in national advertising trades, but we determine our targets read the midwestern trades as well, so we can focus our advertising on that and not waste money on the more expensive national trades that cost so much more and are far less targeted.

Once we've figured out where we want to advertise, we have to decide when and how often. Of course budget will be an issue here. We're just starting out and don't have much of a budget, so we decide to focus our advertising in the fall when we are opening our doors. So here's what we decide:

Media Strategy:

We will do moderate adverising in midwestern advertising journals, focusing heavily on fall issues but keeping an ad in one quarterly journal throughout the year.

Now that we have the basics covered, let's fill in our tactics, and more of the details of our plan, including our desired outcomes and metrics, our timing, and who in our company has project ownership. And remember, let's keep it simple.

Tactics:

1. Do moderate PR in local advertising papers to develop credibility and let people know who we are.

Five press releases by year's end (as needed, dates TBD) on awards won by our top directors and producers, employment releases about top creatives who join our company.

At least two editorial placements by year end:
—Editorial article on Film Noir style, Oct. issue *Video Monthly*
—Editorial article on our best director's award-winning body of work, Nov. *Advertising Style*, Midwestern Edition

TOTAL COST of PR: $20k
Project Owner: P. King

2. Do moderate advertising in local advertising trade papers to entice people to use us by focusing on a unique benefit we offer.

Ad Creation & Production$35k	
—Full page ads in four quarterly issues of *Midwestern Advertising*	$12k
—Full page ads in Oct. and Nov. issues of *Video Monthly*	$6k
—Double spreads Oct. and Nov. issues of *Advertising Style, Midwest Edition*	$5k
TOTAL COST:	$58k

Project Owner: P. King

3. Do a targeted direct mail campaign to introduce company to qualified prospective clients and convert to new clients and significant revenue.

Goal: 10% response rate, 5 new clients, $200k in revenue by 3/15

Purchase lists from	
—*Advertising Style*, Midwest Edition	$2k
—*Video Monthly*, Midwest list	$3k
—*Midwestern Advertising*	$2k
Develop/produce high quality direct mail/promotion ($150 × 200 units)	$30k
Postage	$0.5k
Tracking/conversion	$4.5k
TOTAL COST:	$42k

Project Timing & Ownership:

Develop initial list by 8/1	Owner: L. Stryker
Qualify list by 9/15	Owner: L. Stryker
Create piece by 9/15	Owner: P. King
Send by 10/1	Owner: L. Stryker
Follow up by 10/21	Owner: J. Taylor

Conversion by 12/1 Owner: J. Taylor
Report back on outcomes 3/15 Owner: J. Taylor/P. King

TOTAL COST OF MARKETING COMMUNICATIONS $120k

Create an initial draft of your marketing communications plan, filling in what you can and making note of what you need to do to fill in the gaps.

Hopefully, you can see how these plans flow out from one another. Let's do one more quick plan using our video example.

The Employee Relations Plan

THE VIDEO COMPANY had a strategy to recruit the most talented people in the area.

As you see, this is a selling point for the company, supporting the benefit that you'll get the most original work possible because we have the most talented, creative people. Now, our employee relations plan should be developed to support this. Again, let's start with our vision and our people strategy.

Vision: to be the top video producer of high quality, artistic, stylized video in the tri-state area
High-level strategy: to recruit and retain the most talented creatives in the area.

Now, we have to ask ourselves how we do this. Perhaps we do some research on potential employees. First we have to identify the stars. Then we have to ask them what they want from a job. What would it take to entice them to join us and then keep them happy? Let's say we find out that they need creative freedom, the ability to work with the best equipment and other talented creatives, good clients with good budgets, and lots of vacation time. Hey, guess what, money didn't come up! They don't need more money so much as competitive money. They really want challenge and freedom. Well, then that's what our plan should do.

From here, we would develop objectives and tactics that support this strategy, just as we did with the other plans. Tactics to give employees freedom may include allowing them to design their own job and pick their own team, which will report to them.

Take a stab at developing an employee relations plan for your company, based on your people strategy.

Ten

Building a Community

10. value relationships

What really matters is the people.

At least that's what I hear over and over again, from entrepreneurs running all kinds of businesses in lots of different industries.

It's all about people. The people you serve, your clients, shareholders and/or members of your community who benefit from or are otherwise affected by your company's products, services, and contributions. The people you work with on a daily basis, including employees, partners, and suppliers. The people you care about, like your family, who will benefit from your company's success.

When you start a company, you are creating a community, however small it may be. Every person you invite into this community impacts it. For example, if you work with a supplier with questionable business practices, your people and your clients could be affected, on a physical or energetic basis. You may pay more for an inferior product that is incorrectly labeled, or potential clients may learn you work with this company and your reputation may be sullied. It's hard to be an eagle if you hang with turkeys, to mangle a saying.

On the other hand, if you successfully recruit employees or land clients who are widely respected for their integrity and vision, your company may benefit as potential clients or employees who know and respect these people learn that they have joined you. Or, if you have really great people, your clients and suppliers will realize that through their interactions and think well of your company.

Your Life

Taking Care of Your Personal Network

WE ALL CREATE our own network of friends and acquaintances, by choice, by accident, by birth or geography or convenience. Yet most of us rarely if ever take stock of this network. We need to pay attention to it, like our health or our finances, because it is an absolutely crucial part of our lives.

What is your ideal network of people? What are they like? How do you relate with them?

Who are the people you care about most in the world? For each of them, how do you feel when you're with them? How do they impact how you feel about yourself, if at all? How do they influence you or inspire you?

Who are the people you see most on a daily basis? How do you interact? How do you think they feel about you? How do they make you feel about yourself?

Who would you like to get to know better in your life? Why? What do you like or find attractive or interesting about them?

Is anything missing from your network of people? What is healthy about it? What is unhealthy about it? How would you like to see it change?

What types of people (and/or specific people) would you like to join your network? What types of people (and/or specific people) would you like to see leave your network?

What can you do to make your network of people closer to your ideal?

Fixing What Ails You

Many years ago after moving to a new city, I realized that a few of the new people in my life were actually pretty mean to me on occasion. They would give me backhanded compliments or take advantage of me somehow, and while my feelings would be hurt, I would take it without question and then actually make excuses for them. They didn't mean it, I would tell myself. They didn't realize how it sounded. They're just honest enough to tell me the truth (about how undeserving I was).

Once I recognized the pattern, I decided to try to nip it in the bud. I made a list of the five friends and coworkers who occasionally treated me this way. I sharply confronted one friend the next time she said something passive-aggressively mean, had a long heart-to-heart with another, and cut another one out completely from my life when she stepped too far over the line.

And then I noticed something interesting. The other two people on my list, whom I was watching closely in terms of our interactions but had not yet talked to, changed their tune completely. They didn't know about my realization or my list. And yet things were different. I realized that I must have changed on some level—I was no longer willing to take part in this pattern of interaction—and because of it, my relationships changed on some subconscious (or energetic) level.

The people with whom we choose to spend our time and the ways in which we relate to them say a lot about who we are and impact what we can become.

Are there any negative patterns that you play out repeatedly with people in your life?

What are the negative patterns?

How would you describe the interactions through which the patterns are manifested?

Who are the people that engage in this pattern with you?

If you wanted to change this pattern, what would happen? How would you do it?

Your Company

Attracting the Best People for Your Community

YOU CAN CONSCIOUSLY create your work network to support and reflect your highest ideals. We can help create the community we desire through our intentions. We can try to attract the best people for our purposes.

That means we first have to decide the type of people that we hope to attract, and then we have to ask the universe. And then, we have to selectively judge, pick, and choose each person to the best of our ability.

If you are already in business, describe your typical clients. Include characteristics, values, personalities. If you're not up and running yet, describe what you expect your typical clients to be like.

Now describe your ideal clients. How do these groups differ? Why are they different? Is there any way you can try to find clients who are closer to your ideal?

Write at least a page on what you hope for in terms of ideal clients. When you're done, offer your hopes to the universe and ask for help in attracting the best clients for you.

Now repeat this exercise for each of the following groups that are relevant to your company:

- *Your people*
- *Your partners*
- *Your Board members*
- *Your investors*
- *Your suppliers*

Creating Healthier Patterns

I'VE NOTICED IN my work and in my own life that people create and/or experience patterns in their business relationships in the same way they do in their personal lives (as we discussed in chapter one). For example, if a person finds themselves in abusive personal relationships, they may also experience abusive business partnerships or clients. This makes sense, especially in smaller companies.

One of my clients has difficulty saying no, and some of her family members and friends walk all over her boundaries the same way her clients do. No matter how she tries to limit her hours, she always seems to end up working more. So she plays out her typical behaviors and helps create certain patterns with those people who have complementary behaviors. Another way to look at it is that she is getting more opportunities to overcome her issues and reverse her patterns. However you want to interpret it, it makes sense. Most of us probably do this in our own lives, because we are essentially the same person at work and at home.

If you have an awareness of your issues and the patterns that you tend to create or participate in, you can make conscious decisions about who you want to invite into your community to minimize the impact or reverse the trend. You probably don't want to partner with someone with the same exact issues or, conversely, one who might play into your issues and create a negative pattern between you. Many businesses or groups of people operate like dysfunctional families. And many entrepreneurs find themselves playing part psychiatrist, part mediator, and part police officer. It can be messy.

What were the issues you identified from chapter one? What types of people would play into these issues if they joined your community? How can you avoid letting yourself or your company create this type of pattern? If you notice yourself or your people falling into this type of potential pattern, how will you cut it off at the pass?

Getting in Touch with Your Inner Leader

LEADERSHIP IS A big issue. There are zillions of books about it, and pretty much an infinite number of ways to describe what makes an effective leader. Sure, I have my opinions, and people I respect have their opinions, and there's lots of research that says lots of different things about how you can act as a leader to achieve certain things. But my feelings about what makes effective leadership is that:

1. yes, we did learn a lot of the important stuff about interacting with others in kindergarten, and
2. basically, it depends. What's right for one situation isn't right for another—and a good leader knows the difference and can react differently depending on the context and circumstances.

The way you lead helps shape your culture. Therefore, your leadership style should be informed by the culture you're trying to cultivate.

And of course, the way you lead most effectively depends mostly on who you are. I can say, good leaders have charisma! But what if you don't? (Besides, can you say Bill Gates?) Or I could say, "Effective leaders listen and have compassion!" But Hitler didn't have compassion, and I doubt he was a good listener, but, while he was truly evil, he also was an "effective leader" if your definition of leadership is to influence a whole bunch of people to do what you want them to.

So let's do this together.

Who are some leaders you respect and admire?

What makes each of them good leaders? What about their leadership style makes them successful in leading a certain group? What aspect of their style would you like to emulate?

What kind of a leader do you aspire to be?

What leadership qualities do you have inherently?

What skills do you have that would make you a good leader (e.g., passion, vision, decisiveness, sense of humor, willingness to try that unidentifiable dish first, whatever)?

What kind of culture and community do you hope to create?

How can these qualities and values be reflected and reinforced? (For example, if you want a culture in which people are willing to take risks, then you need to create an environment in which mistakes are expected and tolerated. As a leader, how do you achieve that?)

What skills or qualities do you have that can help you with creating this kind of culture?

How can you further develop or refine these qualities?

Letting People Go

FIRING PEOPLE IS hard. But no matter how hard it is on you, it's undoubtedly even tougher on them. It's important to be careful—legally and emotionally.

The legal aspects of firing someone can be tricky. Always get advice from a lawyer or a trained Human Resources professional before letting someone go, or even discussing that possibility. In some cases, firing someone can be seemingly more difficult than getting a divorce. I once had to document someone's shortcomings for several months and hold weekly progress meetings before letting him go!

The emotional aspects are every bit as—if not more—difficult. Obviously, you don't want to crush the person's self-esteem. It's important to not focus on the person's perceived shortcomings, but rather on the lack of a good fit between the person's capabilities and the requirements for doing a good job. I've found it helpful to comment on all the good things about that person, on all the things they do well, in those final conversations (with a lawyer's prior approval). You also need to be careful when telling candidates why you did not hire them. Be careful—but kind.

Getting Your People to Act Like Owners

ON MORE THAN one occasion, I've encountered entrepreneurs who feel angry or hurt that their people are acting like mere employees. Of course, that's what they are—employees. They may work incredibly hard, they may have a passion to do a good job, they may believe in the business . . . but they will probably never care, or be willing to sacrifice, as much as you do. The future success of your company may matter less to them than other aspects of their own lives, even if they are committed to doing a great job. It makes sense, right?

If you want someone to act like an owner—make them one! Otherwise, you can't really expect people to care as much as you do. This is your dream, not theirs. You can try to teach them to think like an owner, and perhaps to emulate an owner on occasion, but if you want them to truly act like one, you have to put them in that situation. And even then, giving them stock options or a junior partnership or whatever may not do the trick (although it will undoubtedly help) if it is not their life's dream. It's sort of like asking your child's baby-sitter or teacher to act like a parent. Would you really want that?

And if so, are you willing to let them adopt? Are you willing to make them an owner to get them to act like one? This question is a great test for business owners who expect blood, sweat, and tears from their people. Maybe you should just expect sweat, or maybe sweat and passion. Because how can you expect something you're not willing to give? Maybe it's only appropriate—and only fair—that they act like well-compensated, highly motivated employees, if that's the exchange you're willing to make—high compensation in return for their motivation. What investment are you expecting, and how much are you willing to give?

If and when you decide you do want to share ownership with new partners or your people, you may want to discuss and consider their passions and their dreams, because your company will undoubtedly be impacted by the new energy and leadership they will bring to it. Will they take the company in the direction you want it to go, or are you willing to cede a little control because you believe the company will be better served with their input?

How to Say Thank You

ONE OF THE simplest, most effective ways of enhancing your relationships is often the rarest—saying thank you. Here are some things you can do to express your appreciation:

1. BE AWARE.

   Before you can say thank you, you have to know who deserves thanks! As your company gets busier and grows, it can be difficult to stay on top of who's doing what, who's going above and beyond the call of duty, and who is picking up any slack. Keep an eye open for what is going on. Ask your management team or whoever the appropriate people are, to keep you informed about who is doing a particularly good job, from the salesperson who is breaking her neck to land that huge deal to the receptionist who kept his cool with an angry client to the supplier who delivered your order personally on his day off to be sure you got it in time.

2. ACKNOWLEDGE PEOPLE'S WORK.

   As the leader of your company, your words and actions now carry added import. Your people may be paying closer attention than you realize, perhaps even reading into what you do, so be aware. You have to be extra careful.

   The positive side of this is that your attention may mean a lot to your people. Stopping by someone's desk to say, "good job!" or writing a handwritten note to thank someone for staying late last night to get something out the door may go a long way in motivating people and letting them know that they're valued.

   Many suppliers in particular hear the little words "thank you" far too infrequently. We all expect great service, as do our clients, but that doesn't mean it's easy.

   In short, just say it!

3. Give substantive feedback.

Most people appreciate receiving feedback on the work they've done for you. It's disheartening when we work hard on a project and then never find out what people thought of it, or get only superficial or general feedback, like "It was fine." Giving people timely, thorough feedback is a way to show respect, and also, very importantly, to teach them or at least to communicate what you want and expect from them. Even though we're busy, letting someone know what you really liked and what didn't work for you is just good business.

This is especially true for suppliers, who may not see you or hear from you again until the next time you need them. Time is often short, but if you take the time to drop a quick line or make a phone call to let them know what you thought of their work, odds are they will greatly appreciate it.

Another quick thought about giving feedback: if your people have worked hard on a large project, it's probably better not to pick it apart when they're exhausted. Pat them on the back, compliment the things that worked (unless it was a disaster) and then debrief them after they're rested. Huge projects require risks. Some things will work better than others, and such projects will almost never go perfectly. Having a meeting after the fact to openly discuss what worked and what didn't and what you've all learned about how it could be done better in the future, from their perspective as well, is a great way to make it a constructive learning experience that motivates instead of discourages people.

4. Remember that benefits and incentives are not thank-you's.

Companies offer benefits and training to attract and retain good people. Yet, I have noticed that sometimes owners and leaders assume that such benefits should be thanks enough for hard work, and that employees should be grateful. Incentive plans are the same way; if you offer an incentive for someone to do something and they do it, don't expect gratitude. It's an exchange, and they are playing by the rules. If you want to say thank you, it should not be with something that's already a part of what they understand their compensation and benefits package to be. A gift, award or unexpected bonus, however, do say "thank you." They are outside of the agreed-upon exchange, and they work as acknowledgment of going beyond the call of duty in some way.

5. BE SENSITIVE AND THOUGHTFUL.

   The little things aren't always so little! People appreciate thoughtfulness, because it shows you are really paying attention to them. So, instead of just handing out a check or gift or whatever, offer some kind words that will be meaningful to the recipients, or that show that you know who they are and what they care about.

   Also, be sure to present the gift or award in a way they would appreciate. For example, if someone is painfully shy, don't drag him up on stage in front of a hundred people. If someone is going through a divorce, don't send her on a trip for two to Niagara Falls. Also, be sure you always spell and pronounce your employees' names correctly. (I've seen a couple CEOs of big companies whom I greatly respect huddling with their people before presentations at employee meetings practicing the pronunciation of employees' names to make sure they get it perfect. This is not only very kind but also very smart.

6. CELEBRATE TOGETHER.

   Take the time to celebrate hard work and achievements. Have a pizza party! A trip to the local amusement park! This is a quick way to say thanks and also have fun as a team. You work together, why not play together too?

Eleven

FACING THE ABYSS

11. be courageous

ENTREPRENEURS ALMOST BY definition are risk-takers. Creating something new from scratch is a major leap of faith and requires courage. Entrepreneurs, like artists, have to face a steady stream of rejection. The rejections can feel very personal because they deal with things you care deeply about—your baby, your project.

Fear is a fact of life. Just because entrepreneurs are willing to take more risks than most people does not mean that they are immune to fear. In fact, most entrepreneurs I know feel fear much of the time. It just doesn't stop them from following their dream.

Starting a company—especially one that reflects you in a deeply personal way—can be a scary thing. It's scary to take financial risks and leave the steady paycheck behind. It's scary to risk failure. It's scary to express yourself. But, many entrepreneurs agree, life is short: why not have an extraordinary one?

Believe in Yourself

YOU HAVE A dream. A wonderful, ambitious desire. You want to create a company! And yet, the first thing you may get from people around you is negativity. Who the hell do you think you are? Are you crazy? And then you'll probably get the long list of reasons why your idea is bad, why it could never work, all the risks and problems and nightmares that will probably befall you.

One client, who is in the very earliest stages of creating a new company, said, "I thought I learned to deal with rejection after years of being in sales, but it's even harder when you're dealing with rejection of your own ideas. A friend of mine always tells me a majority of small businesses go bankrupt in the first year, and even though I don't know where he gets that information, a lot of times I take him at his word. My dream could stop there, but the key is not listening to someone else but listening to your heart and finding a way to make it happen."

I don't know why people insist on pointing out all the difficulties of starting a business. This is the time when you most need support! You are doing a courageous and exciting thing . . . but many entrepreneurs are greeted with negativity from people they love and respect. This negativity is a painful rejection of your dream, your excitement, and your ability to make it happen.

Let's be honest. Nobody likes to be rejected. Rejection sucks!

Well, get used to it, because you're going to have to learn to deal with it. You're going to hear a lot of no's. You're going to hear no's when you care, no's when you don't care, no's when you think you've been kicked to the ground as low as you can go. And then you're going to pick yourself up and hear no again.

It's OK. That's just part of it. If you haven't learned it already, you're going to have to learn to let it roll off your back, or to feel the pain and then let go and move on. As one client said, "Rejection is like gravel on bare feet. In the beginning of the summer, after a winter of shoes and socks, feet are vulnerable and tender. It's a painful experience to be outside and barefoot. Toward the end of the summer, the gravel and sand toughens you up. Your feet don't hurt anymore when you walk outside without shoes. This is the same with rejection. The more you get, the tougher you get. I used to say, 'Oh, I can't stand the thought of one more rejection.' Now I say, 'Bring it on.'"

The good thing about rejection is that it is survivable, with the right frame of mind and a little practice. And there are lots of ways to deal with it.

Your Life

Dealing with Rejection

IF YOU FEAR it, you better believe it will come.

One of the rejections I feared most growing up was not getting into a certain well-known school, where many of our family friends and relatives, including both of my parents, had gone. From an early age, I developed an unrelenting fear, which was completely internally generated, that I wouldn't get in. Did I actually want to go there? I don't even know, because that was never the question. For years, it was like a haunting refrain in my little, screwed-up brain: "What if I don't get in? What if I don't? What if everyone else does and I don't?"

I didn't have to face that rejection in high school because I ended up finding the right college for me and going early decision, which meant I never had to apply anywhere else and go through the torture the rest of my classmates went through. Phew! I'm not sure I could have dealt with it then. And then I applied to one graduate school out of college for my master's, and went there.

I didn't get off that easy, though. Years later, in my twenties, I applied to several schools, including the one in question, to get a Ph.D. I thought a lot before I applied there, given its past sway over me, and having lived quite happily up to that point without having to answer the scary question of whether or not I could get in. But I decided I might as well find out once and for all. . . . So I applied.

I heard from almost every other school first, and I had some good, comparable options (thank God). But then one day, the scary, skinny letter arrived from the department to which I was applying at the school in question. The day had arrived. The rejection was here at last! I carried the envelope up the elevator to my apartment, where I stared at it for twenty minutes before I could open it.

Now the beautiful part of this story was that it wasn't just a typical rejection. It was a doozy! I wish I had saved the letter, so I could quote it word for word, but to paraphrase from memory, it began with the usual "we regret to inform you" sentence, followed by something like: "In fact, we rejected many candidates far more qualified than you!" And it kept going from there.

I had to read it six or seven times before I could believe it. I mean, I knew the rejection was real, but to rub my nose in it, kick me when I'm down? Had a disgruntled intern written this letter? Surely, this couldn't be the department's form rejection letter. Or, oh God, had they cooked this one up special, just for me? Finally, I had to laugh. It couldn't be a more perfect response to my fear. And I called my parents and my friends and read them the letter, and they were as shocked as I was, but then they laughed with me. The fact that the rejection was so harsh actually removed the sting, in some weird way. It made me laugh at myself and the situation, because it was clearly the most appropriate answer to what I most feared, so ridiculously, for so many years. And I lived.

What are the worst rejections you've ever lived through, personally or professionally?

How did you do it? What did you learn?

What are some positive ways you deal with rejection?

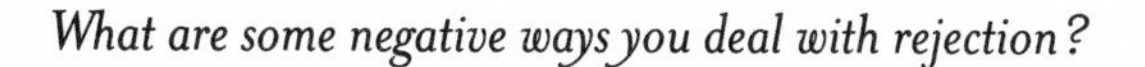

What are some negative ways you deal with rejection?

Do you have any patterns in dealing with rejection?

Can you think of an example of someone you know who dealt with a rejection well? How did they do it? What did you learn from them?

Embracing Rejection

WE CAN HELP each other deal with rejection in healthy ways.

One theater in Chicago offered discounted admission to all actors or writers upon presentation of a rejection letter! I know a lot of people who went just so they could make use of those letters.

In my high school, an insanely difficult college prep school filled with academic type A's such as myself, the sunny Houston winter senior year was a dark and terrifying time. College rejections were coming, each one a crushing blow.

"Senior Country," a huge, couch-filled room where seniors hung out between classes, had one whole wall made of windows. People started to bring college rejection letters to school and hang them on the wall of windows, often to scattered applause from the other students present. It was actually a pretty supportive thing, and it pulled us together in our mutual fear and empathy. I remember one guy in our class marching in one Monday morning and hanging rejection letters on the window. He must have had seven or eight, all at once. Our worst fear, realized! The applause and empathetic laughter just kept growing as he taped up the letters. He finished his task to a standing ovation, and took a bow. Everyone felt a whole lot better.

Friends help, too. I have two different writing groups who understand rejection. We help each other recognize the value in getting our work out there regardless of the response, get indignant on each other's behalf at nasty rejections, and celebrate the good rejections. And we really celebrate victories, large and small!

Here's what one of my writer friends says about rejection: "It takes a lot of courage to let go of your work and send it out to the universe. Getting letters back, even if they're only rejection letters, means somebody out there has seen and considered your work. It's better to get SOME type of response than to have your work gather dust in a desk drawer somewhere. Plus, I now believe wholeheartedly that the right opportunity will present itself at the right time."

Another friend of mine, an artist and filmmaker, says "GET USED TO IT! Ninety-five percent of the time it's not a reflection of your abilities or talent, but a matter of a combination of arbitrary circumstances. Definitely don't let it stop you because it's often a disguise for what you really doubt about yourself. It's proof that you have been exposing your creations to the world and that you have guts."

Using It to Inspire You

SOME PEOPLE ARE motivated by rejection to prove others wrong—like Michael Jordan, who didn't make the varsity basketball team when he was a sophomore in high school. It inspired him to work even harder—and boy did he show them!

One client says, "I keep all of my rejection letters in a big file, tucked away. This way, I don't have to look at the file. But I know it's there. It spurs me on. Someday all the people gathered in my file will be sorry they rejected me."

Blowing It Off

I'VE NOTICED THAT when people are confident or experienced, they can actually shake off rejection as if it didn't even happen. I learned a valuable lesson about this from a friend and colleague who is a well-known freelance advertising creative. I was hired to write an awards show a couple years ago for the advertising industry. I hired my friend to write the comedic aspects and host banter of the show. Two well-known players in the industry were lined up to host the show. My friend, who is also a brilliant comedian, wrote some great bits for the script. We worked hard and pulled everything together. The hosts seemed very confident and felt they didn't need to rehearse. I believed them.

The night of the show, the hosts showed up cocky and very possibly a little toasted. I felt secure in the knowledge that they had a good script, thanks mainly to my funny friend and cowriter, who was not attending the show. However, from the moment they took the stage, it was a disaster. They tried to wing it, and then when no one laughed, they went back to the script in the middle, so the jokes had no setup and made no sense. Through the night, it went from bad to worse, and they got embarrassed and became bitter. They started completely and repeatedly dissing the script and the writers, namely me and my cowriter. I dreaded the end of the show when our names were spread across the huge screen for everyone who was anyone in the advertising community to see. It was humiliating, but I felt far worse for my cowriter, who was extremely well known in that community and made his living among these people. He couldn't just disappear for a while like I wanted to.

I called him early the next morning to let him know what had happened, hoping to reach him before one of his advertising friends did. When I explained what had occurred, he said, "Oh, it happens. I've had scripts butchered before and I'm sure I will again."

And he really meant it. He couldn't have been more unconcerned. I was amazed and impressed. This confidence is one reason why he's now succeeding as a playwright and starting to make a name for himself in Hollywood.

Feeling the Pain—Then Letting It Go

ANYONE WHO CREATES lives with rejection. As an entrepreneur or artist, it's almost a daily thing. You get used to it. There are good rejections and bad rejections. There are good days and bad days. Most of the time, the rejections are just part of it, just a numbers game. And then there are the bone-crushing rejections that really hurt out of all proportion.

One client suffered a particularly painful rejection after a long consideration process. She said, "I went into our tiny laundry room, threw myself down on the floor near the litter box, and cried for nearly an hour. I kept thinking over and over in my mind, 'It's never going to be me. I will never be the one who's picked for something like this.' It took a while to dig out the cat litter that had ground into my kneecaps!"

Sometimes you have to grieve—but then you let it go. How?

Friends and mentors come in handy to help you deal with rejection. Lauren, an architect, says, "You can spread the weight of rejection by talking with people you value about the whole denouement, just as you can help carry a floor load by adding more joists to the floor structure. The load is still there but you don't feel it as much because you have joists at every twelve inches instead of every two feet."

"Rejection is like getting splattered all over the pavement by a Mack truck," says Jen, an artist and business owner. "I have become quite used to rejection over time and simply move through it, though the level of disappointment is the same every time. First I wander around taking it personally and feeling discouraged. Then I do things to gain perspective, which usually entail talking to people in my support network—family, friends, mentors. Also, I write about it and read inspirational books."

You can also be a friend to yourself in these situations. You can choose to be as supportive of yourself as you would be of a friend, and say positive things to yourself. As another client says, "Even after all this time, I still take rejection personally sometimes. But I use a lot of self-talk to get over it, like 'OK, put it behind you, keep moving.' I try to stay focused on my goal and my purpose."

Learning from Artists

WORKING ARTISTS OFTEN get pretty good at rejection. While rejections may still be painful, many artists learn how to work with it. Below, a singer and composer explains how he used a painful rejection to his advantage. This may be helpful as you begin to design your company.

The best thing you can do with rejection is to first acknowledge the pain of it. Once you can see past that, find out if there's anything to be learned from it. It also helps to talk about it with people whom you trust.

A year ago, I was teaching a class called "The Art of Success" and right before class I heard that my demo had been reviewed in that week's *Music Connection*. Before class I ran over to the newsstand to get a copy, and the review stunk. All through class I was kind of sad and freaked out. Here I'm teaching a class on how to define success for yourself and I got this horrible review. A half hour before class was ending, I shared the review with them and told them how I was still kind of raw from it, and it was very helpful for me and for them, I think. I read the review out loud all the way through. The class's first response was "that wasn't so bad! From what you'd said, I expected them to hate it."

I was prepared for criticisms of my music as being too deep for radio, (There was a song about the murder of Matthew Shepard and another about a transsexual friend of mine named Joanne.) But they said my lyrics were too shallow. They also said that "Joanne" was about a good girl gone bad, which is clearly just plain wrong. They had reviewed another demo of mine and said that my lyrics are a cut above the rest of the genre's. I don't want to change the way I write lyrics. I like them the way they are. Bottom line: They didn't get it and didn't want to get it.

The first thing I asked myself was "Are there at least a few quotes I can use from this review for my press packet?" Not really. "Serviceable voice!!!" Doesn't exactly make the labels jump to the phone. At the end of class, I played the demo for the class . I wanted to crawl into a hole but I forced myself to play it and they had nothing but praise for it.

So what can I learn from this? I had incorrectly assumed that the music reviewer would listen to the songs and analyze them critically, but that's not how it happens. More often than not, it's somebody that listens to the tunes (maybe while they are doing something else) and they take a cursory look through the packet. I need to facilitate their job if I can. Now I add a little one sentence blurb about what the song is about. I'm a lot clearer and it makes for less misunderstanding. My press packet is better because of the crappy review.

Some more thoughts:

1) Not everyone is going to like everything. Are you asking someone who hates rock music (like my mom) to listen to your garage band and expecting her to fall in love with it? Unrealistic. Also, some people just don't give praise easily. That's okay. They may really like it, but they just aren't demonstrative about it. Take what you can get.

2) Don't open yourself up to criticism that will do you no good. If my mom likes your rock music, you've probably done something wrong. Likewise, if you have a friend who is always hurtful in the way they criticize, either shelter your project from them or wait until you're feeling really confident.

3) Don't open yourself up to criticism until you're ready for it. When I've just finished a song, I always think it's the best song ever written and I need that period of euphoria. Then a day later I can be more objective and hear someone say they don't like the bridge.

4) Be clear about why you need the criticism. Are you wanting an overall view or are you looking for something specific? There is a time for either one. If you're in the beginning stages of a song, an overall impression of a respected friend with fresh ears can be invaluable. Let them know where you are in the process. If you aren't finished with the mixing of the tracks, someone telling you that your voice needs to be louder won't really help. You were going to do that anyway. Maybe you need them to respond to the songwriting because you're going to redo the

vocals later. If your demo is finished and all the artwork is done, then maybe you want someone listening to tell you if they know a record label you should send it to that does your kind of music.

5) If you ask for criticism, get prepared for criticism. Constructive criticism can make your project better. Sometimes we don't want to hear it. We want them to say it was perfect and everyone in the world will love it. Unrealistic, but a lot of people (me, too sometimes) ask for criticism when we really want reassurance. Reassurance is great, but good criticism is not always going to be reassuring. Be clear what you're looking for and don't be afraid to ask for it.

6) If someone gives you a compliment it can mean a lot of things. It can mean "I love it." It can mean "I like it a little, but I want to encourage you." It can mean "I hate it, but I'm too nice/too busy/too much of a jerk to tell you." Whatever. Take compliments like you take criticism: with a grain of salt. It's just one person with one opinion whether they love it or hate it. If you think they aren't being fully honest with you, ask a follow-up question that lets them know that you are really trying to make this a better project and aren't just looking for reassurance.

7) As I said before, find out what you can use from the criticism. For instance, why do people submit a demo for review in a magazine? To generate some music industry attention. Therefore, a review that says "The guitar sounds like a chainsaw, the songs were unlistenable, but luckily she sings like an angel." can look great in a sheet of press clippings. ". . . she sings like an angel." —*Rolling Stone Magazine.* Find the silver lining. Naturally it would be better if the whole review was fantastic, but take what you can get.

Doug Wood

Singer, composer

Your Company

Preparing for Rejection

HERE ARE SOME of the people who may reject your new baby in some way:

1. friends and family
2. investors
3. banks
4. suppliers
5. potential customers
6. the media
7. potential employees

It's very possible that you will experience rejection—perhaps a great deal of rejection—from one or more of these groups of people.

One great way to deal with rejection is to be prepared for it. If you have a positive answer handy to respond to negativity and rejection, even if it's only for yourself, you can shield yourself from some of the pain. For example, if you have an answer ready for a comment (unsubstantiated, by the way), "Ninety percent of all businesses go bankrupt the first year," you can just say back (or to yourself), "Then I'll be one of the ten percent who makes it!"

Another way is to develop a perspective in which rejection is not a crushing blow. If I'm up for a project with other people, I always ask for the best thing for everyone to happen. If I don't get it, I tell myself that something better is coming. And I try to remove my attachment to being chosen, to winning, and ask myself if this is truly a good fit, and if it's a project I even want. I firmly believe things will work out for the best.

I've also found that people have difficulty separating themselves from their company. I can understand that, especially since I espouse creating very personal companies. And yet, the ability to differentiate is crucial to your well-being. The most important thing is to not take things personally.

I had one client who took everything incredibly personally. If he did not win a piece of business—even if he didn't lose to a competitor but the business just went away due to timing or budget—he was devastated. If a prospective client he had cold-called did not return his call within a day, he took it as a personal affront. A negative comment could send him into a tailspin for days. By the same token, when a client complimented him or gave him some work, he was thrilled and took it as a comment on his value as a person.

Needless to say, he was up and down like a yo-yo. He wasted a lot of energy this way, and created a lot of trauma for himself and for everyone around him. It was obviously a personal issue reflected throughout his life, but it was a good reminder of how important it is to keep perspective. No one client, or deal, or check is responsible for our security or reflects on our value as a person; instead, it comes from something greater.

Staying centered is crucial. And one way to do that is to be aware of your own personal patterns in responding to rejection, and to watch out for them in your business life.

How are you at taking rejection? What coping mechanisms do you use?

Have you been met by negativity from people close to you? How did you handle it? Did you learn from it? How could you have handled it better? Did it stick with you?

Have you experienced any rejection about your company, from investors or mentors or others? How did you deal with it? What did you learn from it?

Come up with a couple alternatives for dealing with this rejection. How could you have dealt with it better? How would you deal with it next time?

List some of the negative comments and rejections you've received, and develop an empowering, affirming response to each of those rejections. What are all the good reasons for your company to exist?

Create affirmations, or positive statements, that support your belief in yourself and your success. Try to repeat the affirmation to yourself as often as you can.

How to Create a Peer Support Group

AS YOU CREATE your own company, you will need a great deal of support. Many entrepreneurs have gotten a great deal of value from mentors. I myself have seen people experience great results from the support of their peers. I am a firm believer in the power of the support group. Here's how you create one for yourself.

1. FIND THE RIGHT PEOPLE.

   The most important thing is to surround yourself with the right people. You'll want your group to be full of people who are undertaking the same type of projects as your are, and who are positive, supportive, trustworthy, and smart. They should be people you trust, whose opinions you may not always agree with but that you always respect. You'll want your fellow group members to be able to interact with each other skillfully and well—no behavior problems! You don't need that kind of headache.

2. DECIDE WHAT YOU WANT FROM THE GROUP.

   Every group member should decide what he or she personally would like to get out of the group. All members should discuss their desires for the group openly and see if they can all come to agreement. If not, this is not the right group for you.

   I was in one group with two other women who were peers in that we all had our own businesses and our creative pursuits. Our meetings covered many aspects of our lives, not just the business or the personal aspects. We would talk about how we felt and how we were doing personally, physically, emotionally and spiritually as well as professionally. This tiny, holistic group was one of the most helpful, supportive groups with which I've ever been involved.

3. SET GUIDELINES AND STICK TO THEM OR ADAPT THEM.

   The group should decide together all the logistics (timing, location, and scheduling), the agenda, and the ground rules for meetings. I have found that meetings function more effectively and efficiently if they are not mixed with socializing but are kept strictly business (you can socialize with people at a different time!). Also, I've found that it's best to keep to a general outline and schedule.

4. COVER NOT ONLY YOUR ISSUES, BUT ALSO COMMIT TO GOALS AND CELEBRATE YOUR SUCCESSES.

   Definitely incorporate feedback into your agendas. It's helpful to share challenges and allow plenty of time for the rest of the group to offer suggestions and thoughts about how to handle it. Don't forget to share all of the good things that happened since the last meeting, and all of the things that you did that you are proud of, and make sure you schedule time for the group to respond. We don't pat ourselves on the back often enough! Also, commit to what you want to achieve before the next meeting.

5. HAVE FUN!

   This meeting should be enjoyable, as well as affirming and helpful. Find a pleasant place to meet, keep the meetings short enough so they don't become a bore and frequent enough so that they're helpful without becoming a chore. And be sure to celebrate successes!

KEEPING THE FAITH

12. work with the universe

WHEN ALL IS said and done, at some point you're doing all you can do, and you have to trust the universe. You can't control it, but you can learn to work with it.

Ask for Help

A FEW YEARS ago, I took a class on creating abundance. As homework, we were asked to come up with something we wanted but couldn't afford. I had four things I wanted: a laptop; a sideboard for my dining room that went with my table; a washing machine so I could stop going to the laundromat; and a trip to Europe. I settled on the laptop.

Our homework was to ask the universe for the thing we wanted, and then to let it come to us without forcing it or buying it ourselves. It seemed pretty hard to imagine, but I did it.

A few days later, I was asked to join a team to work on an acquisition in Europe. A runner-up had come true! Then, the next week, my landlord told me she had purchased a washing machine for the building, and I could use it if I paid twenty dollars a month for the water. Great! It was cheaper than buying a whole new one, and also unexpected.

A couple weeks after that, my parents came into town for the wedding of a family friend. One afternoon, we were walking down Michigan Avenue, and my mother walked into a furniture store.

"This is where I got my dining room table," I told her. She walked past it later, and stopped by the accompanying sideboard.

"This is nice," she said.

"Yeah, I'm hoping to get it someday," I told her.

She bought it for me, on a whim, on the spot. I was shocked! All the runners-up had come true, all unexpectedly, without any effort on my part. How would my laptop come to me? Now it was just a matter of waiting to find out.

A couple weeks later, I gave notice to my job that I was leaving and began to set up my own little company. One day I got a card from my parents (very generous agents of the universe!). Inside it was an unexpected and unsolicited check for some money to "set up an office," including computer, printer, and fax machine! Way more than I had even asked for. I was amazed.

A grand slam! The universe had outdone itself.

(Incidentally, the acquisition was pushed back so I never went on the Europe trip through work because I left. I thought about how my clean sweep of creative abundance from the universe had not totally come through. A few months later, a close friend of mine called to say she was moving to London, had tons of frequent-flyer miles, and would I go with her to help get set up in her new home for a few days? Free flight, free place to stay, a whole week with a great friend? That was so preferable to a working trip. I was all over it.)

I once needed to find a new apartment quickly. It was a difficult time of year to find a place in Chicago—the winter. I decided to try the same thing I had done with the abundance class. I made a list of everything I wanted in my apartment.

"French doors," I wrote in gold ink in my journal. "Lots of windows and sunlight. A cool landlord. Lots of cafés nearby where I can write. At least one good new friend in the neighborhood. A gym within walking distance. A bagel place. A juice bar. Lots of parking. Churchbells and trees outside my window. A way to close off the kitchen from the rest of the apartment (to keep the cats out). Two bedrooms within my price range. Built-in bookshelves." I filled the whole page, even listing the two neighborhoods I wanted. Then I wrote a request to the universe to help me find the perfect home for me quickly and easily.

The next day I picked up a paper and circled a bunch of places. I made appointments to see two of them. I stopped by one apartment, but it was too close to a major road. Ten minutes later, I stopped by my second appointment. A friend of mine, who knew about my list, came with me.

The second we entered the apartment, I fell in love with it. It was gorgeous! Windows everywhere. A fireplace and a whole wall of built-in bookshelves. French doors framing a sunroom. A kitchen with a door closing it off from the rest of the apartment. As we were remarking on how perfect it was, church bells rang.

"If there's a café nearby, I'm taking it," I said, as we drove away. On the next block, we passed no less than three cafés and a bagel shop. I took the apartment.

I wasn't even upset that there was no gym in the neighborhood because everything else was perfect. Four months later, I saw a sign in the window of a large space a block away, announcing a health club under construction. I work out there to this day. And they have a great juice bar with fresh juices and smoothies!

Ask for the things or opportunities you really want. Make a list of wishes, ask the universe for its help, and keep your eyes open.

Surrender Control

A FRIEND OF mine decided she wanted to go to medical school. She had her heart set on a specific traditional medical school, but was also accepted to a nearby osteopathic medical school. When she was wait-listed at the school she most wanted to attend, she began to consider the osteopathic program more seriously. After visiting the school and talking with students and professors, she realized that she liked the school and approach better than the traditional one and chose to attend. Now, midway through the program, she is thankful and relieved she chose osteopathic medicine, as she feels she is happier and far better suited to the osteopathic approach than a more traditional one.

Here's something I've seen a lot: a client desperately wants a piece of business. They do everything possible to get that business, including staying up all night worrying and lowering their fees to where they'll barely break even on the deal. But no matter how hard they try, no matter what they do, they can't get that business. Then, suddenly, another, far better deal falls into their lap from out of the blue—and if they had the other piece of business, they would never have gotten or been able to take the new, preferable deal! Once again, it comes down to recognizing why something just isn't working.

Can you think of a time when you really, really wanted something, big or small, and you didn't get it at first or at all, or in the way you expected it, but then it turned out even better than you could have dreamed?

Your Life

Recognizing Miracles in Your Life

MIRACLES HAPPEN ALL the time. They happen in medicine, they happen in traffic, they happen in basketball . . . they happen everywhere. The key is recognizing them. Although sometimes it's more obvious than others.

Here's a pretty big miracle that happened to my friend and client, Ella Leya. Tragically, her son died of leukemia a few years ago at the age of nine. After his death, she was deeply depressed for a long time. She took a trip to Hawaii a year or so after his death. While at a bird sanctuary, she had a spiritual experience where she felt her soul was flying with the birds, over the blue water, and she felt her son's presence very strongly and knew that he was fine, that his spirit was soaring.

After a few hours, she left the sanctuary, feeling more peaceful than she had in a long time. When she and her husband got in their rented car and turned it on, the radio was on, although they both swore it had been off. The song "Free as a Bird" by John Lennon and performed by the Beatles came on and played all the way through. My friend and her husband were shocked. When the song ended, the radio was silent. It had not been on after all.

My friend Bruce had a big miracle too—actually a series of miracles. His son Mark was in a car accident a couple of years ago. His aorta was torn, and time was of the essence. Through a series of "coincidences" and "lucky accidents" the ambulance came on the scene almost immediately and took Mark to a different hospital than it usually would have, where the only surgeon in the area who was expert in dealing with Mark's type of injury worked. Although he was not working, he happened to be close to the hospital at the moment he was paged, walked right into surgery, and saved Mark's life, already against the odds.

Bruce and his wife, Cindy, were told that even if Mark survived his other injuries, he'd almost certainly be paralyzed from the waist down, as they had to shut off the blood flow for a long time to repair the aorta. For days, Mark showed no response or movement in his legs and feet. The doctors had basically given up hope, although they allowed that Mark was already a miracle case so they declined to speculate on the odds of another miracle. And one day, far past the cutoff given by doctors for any expectation of recovery, Mark moved his foot. It's been a long road, but today he's walking again without a cane, appearing in plays and musicals and attending college.

Now those are serious miracles!

What miracles have you experienced in your life?

Create an affirmation about accepting positive miracles in your life, and repeat it to yourself as often as you can. Then be aware of the positive things that happen!

Your Company

Look for the Open Window

WHEN YOU GO into business for yourself, especially in the beginning, you may really begin to feel the flow of the universe. And sometimes that's flow as in "*ebb* and flow." Doors close with no warning and then, just as the fear takes over, a window opens.

When I first left my full-time corporate job (after two years of working up the courage to walk away), I came right back to one of our venture companies as a consultant working twenty hours a week implementing an integrated marketing communications plan I had already created. It was a safe and secure (or perhaps illusionary) way to jump into the consulting world, as I knew everybody, understood the industry and the politics, and had already proven myself.

After several months of enjoying my safe project and my newfound freedom, I ran into an acquaintance at a Saturday-morning fitness class who asked for my help on a proposal and new-business presentation due by Monday. Although I had been looking forward to my weekend off, I helped her out. That Monday morning, I walked into my office at the venture company only to find out it was shutting down due to a sudden decision from on high, and we were all out of jobs (me, immediately). Shocked, I gathered my things and went home—only to find a message from my acquaintance that she had gotten the business and wanted to hire me as a consultant twenty hours a week starting immediately! Phew.

Go with the Flow

A COUPLE OF years into my business, I had developed several steady clients. My biggest problem was that I was taking on too much work. Suddenly, in late summer, all of my projects temporarily dried up, unexpectedly and at the same time, for a variety of reasons, from clients' vacations to budget issues to personnel changes. I found myself with an absolutely open schedule, with no work in sight.

I decided there must be a reason that everything dried up at once. I meditated, asking the universe for some insight. I waited. And waited. Nothing. Suddenly, the phone rang. It was a friend of mine asking me to lunch. Like many people I knew, he was planning to leave his job and wanted some help developing his own company.

Over lunch, I outlined the process I took clients through to develop their marketing plans and corporate identities, taking him through examples of completed programs I had done for various clients and leaving behind some materials for him to work through on his own. Driving home, I realized that I had been taking lots of people through my process. Then it hit me—I'd turn it into a book!

I developed the proposal, wrote a sample chapter, and compiled a list of appropriate literary agents. It took me exactly two weeks. As I was labeling the packages to send to the agents, my phone started to ring. My clients were ready for me to come back—immediately, if not sooner! And those proposals, which took only two weeks of my life, turned into this book.

On occasion, I have been in or seen situations in which I or one of my clients has really wanted a client or a project or a particular outcome, and we have been basically banging our heads against the wall to make it happen. In these situations, it's really important to be clear and able to access your own intuition, which will tell you either to quit that silly headbanging and turn around to see the other opportunity right behind you, or to keep going even though it may seem insane. Do whatever your intuition tells you. Sometimes, for whatever reason, a client relationship ends or a project fails or goes to a competitor. Sometimes companies fail. In fact, many entrepreneurs have had several failures before they hit on the idea that is the one. Listen to your intuition, learn from it, and move on.

Being on my own, I realize how little control I have over projects and work. I have learned to trust the universe, and when doors slam in my face, to trust and work and wait expectantly for the open window.

Trust the Universe

KEVIN GAY BEGAN Morningstar Theater Company by putting up a play he loved. Even though it was a great deal of work, he commented on the flow he experienced:

> "Putting up the play was one of the most exhausting and beautiful events in my life. So many kind and talented people offered their time and help. It was not without stumbling blocks. Early on I lost a lead actor and had to push the opening back two months. What I remember most is sitting down at the beginning and making five phone calls a day to find a theater space. There were days that making those calls were the last thing I wanted to do, but I just had to start walking. In a short time, the perfect space was found and that was just the beginning of the seemingly endless supply of support I received in the process. I learned, actually, to expect that I would be supported. That props would show up, that money would be available. And I was not disappointed."

Ask for what you need, and do the legwork, but let the universe dazzle you with its resourcefulness!

Have you experienced any flow or miracles with your company yet?
If so, what happened?

What are the things you want and need from the universe to help your company?
Write a list of specifically what you want from the universe for your company. Then keep a journal to capture synchronicities, coincidences, and miracles big and small.

How to Get in Tune with the Universe

1. MEDITATE EVERY DAY.

   Meditating is how you tune in to the universe through your own inner voice. It entails quieting your mind and just listening. It is the absolute foundation for spiritual practice. Try to do it every day, even if it's just for five minutes. It's all about training your mind.

   Meditation comes more naturally to some than to others, and it requires patience. It took me two years of meditating before I could actually get past my busy mind . . . but it was worth it. If you have trouble meditating or have never done it, try meditating with a group, through a class or religious or spiritual group. Group meditations are often more powerful. Or you could try meditation tapes or tapes of chants. Whatever it takes, do it! Meditation is the most important tool you can have.

2. ASK THE UNIVERSE FOR HELP.

   Whatever your concept of God or the universe is, you have to ask for help. Throw it out there!

3. LOOK FOR SIGNS OF THAT HELP OR SUPPORT.

   After you ask, you need to be on the lookout for answers to your wish or prayer. It may not come in the form you expect, so look closely. If you have a question, ask—and then look for signs or answers, and, above all, listen to your own intuition.

4. ACKNOWLEDGE SIGNS, SUPPORT, AND MIRACLES, BIG AND SMALL.

   When you do get a response from the universe, acknowledge it! Tell someone, write it down. Be grateful. Say thank you, out loud, in prayer or in a gratitude journal. If you accept help, it keeps coming.

5. WRITE DOWN YOUR DREAMS.

Dreams are a great way to get insight. Pay attention to your dreams and what they may be trying to tell you. It helps to keep a pad of paper by your bed to jot your dreams down as soon as you have them so you don't forget.

6. LOOK FOR THE OPEN WINDOWS.

When something bad happens, learn from it. Try to recognize any recurring patterns. Is the universe trying to teach you something? Why not try to learn it so you can move on? If something bad happens, try to look for the open window. Once again, pay attention!

7. DO AFFIRMATIONS.

Affirmations, thinking positively, and strongly intending or believing can help you work with the universe to create what you want. Write an affirmation like, "The universe is supporting my positive dreams and goals," and say it over and over to yourself. This is a great way to counteract all those negative, self-defeating beliefs and thoughts we may hear and say to ourselves without realizing it.

8. KEEP A JOURNAL.

For many people (and I'm definitely one of them), writing in a journal can be a helpful way to tap into your own intuition and subconscious. If you don't edit yourself, but instead write quickly in stream-of-consciousness for a few pages every day, you may be surprised at what wisdom ends up on the page! Try it before you knock it; it just may work for you too.

ENLIGHTENING MATERIAL

The Artist's Way: A Spiritual Path to Higher Creativity, by Julia Cameron (New York: Penguin Putnam, Inc., 1992).

Ben & Jerry's Double-Dip: How to Run a Values-Led Business and Make Money Too, by Ben Cohen and Jerry Greenfield (New York: A Fireside Book by Simon & Schuster, Inc., 1997).

Built to Last: Successful Habits of Visionary Companies, by James C. Collins and Jerry I. Porras (New York: HarperCollins, 1997).

Business as Unusual: The Triumph of Anita Roddick, by Anita Roddick (New York: Thorsons/HarperCollins, 2000).

Business the Jack Welch Way: 10 Secrets of the World's Greatest Turnaround King, by Stuart Crainer (New York: AMACOM, American Management Association, 1999).

Busines the Richard Branson Way: 10 Secrets of the World's Greatest Brand-Builder, by Des Dearlove (New York, AMACOM, American Management Association, 1999).

Control Your Destiny or Someone Else Will, by Noel M. Tichy and Stratford Sherman (New York: Currency and Doubleday, 1993).

Corporate Cultures: The Rites and Rituals of Corporate Life, by Terrence E. Deal and Allan A. Kennedy (Cambridge, MA: Perseus Books, 2000).

The Corporate Mystic: A Guidebook for Visionaries With Their Feet on the Ground, by Gay Hendricks, Ph.D., and Kate Ludeman, Ph.D. (New York: Bantam Books, 1996).

Creating Money: Keys to Abundance, by Sanaya Roman (Tiburon, CA: H. J. Kramer Inc., Publishers, 1988).

Creative Visualization: Use the Power of Your Imagination to Create What You Want in Your Life, by Shakti Gawain (New York: New World Library, 1995).

Emotional Branding: How Successful Brands Gain the Irrational Edge, by Daryl Travis (Roseville, CA: Prima Publishing, 2000).

Emotional Branding: The New Paradigm for Connecting Brands to People, by Marc Gobe (New York: All Worth Press, 2001).

Forbes: Great Minds of Business, edited by Gretchen Morgenson (New York: John Wiley & Sons, 1997).

The Four Agreements: A Toltec Wisdom Book, by Don Miguel Ruiz, M.D. (San Rafael, CA: Amber-Allen Publishing, 1997).

The Guru Guide: The Best Ideas of the Top Management Thinkers, by Joseph H. Boyett and Jimmie T. Boyett (New York: John Wiley & Sons, Inc., 1998).

The Guru Guide to Entrepreneurship: A Concise Guide to the Best Ideas from the World's Top Entrepreneurs, by Joseph H. Boyett and Jimmie T. Boyett (New York: John Wiley & Sons, Inc., 2001).

Harvests of Joy: How the Good Life Became Great Business, by Robert Mondavi (New York: Harcourt Brace & Co., 1999).

Humanity Wins: A Strategy for Progress & Leadership in Times of Change, by Reinhard Mohn (New York: Crown Publishing Group, 2000).

Jack Welch Speaks: Wisdom from the World's Greatest Business Leader, by Janet Lowe (New York: John Wiley & Sons, Inc., 1998).

Jamming: The Art and Discipline of Business Creativity, by John Kao (New York: Harper-Collins, 1996).

Leadership Is an Art, by Max DePree (New York: Dell Publishing, 1989).

Leading with Soul: An Uncommon Journey of Spirit, by Lee G. Bolman and Terrence E. Deal (San Francisco: Jossey-Bass Publishers, 1995).

Living with Joy: Keys to Personal Power and Spiritual Tranformation, by Sanaya Roman (Tiburon, CA: H. J. Kramer Inc., Publishers, 1986).

Managing from the Heart, by Hyler Bracey et al. (New York: Dell Publishing, 1990).

Man's Search for Meaning: An Introduction to Logotherapy, by Viktor E. Frankl (New York, Simon & Schuster, Inc., 1984).

The Path: Creating Your Mission Statement for Work and for Life, by Laurie Beth Jones (New York: Hyperion, 1996).

Pour Your Heart into It: How Starbucks Built a Company One Cup at a Time, by Howard Schultz and Dori Jones Yang (New York: Hyperion, 1997).

Principle-Centered Leadership, by Stephen R. Covey (New York: A Fireside Book by Simon & Schuster, Inc., 1992).

The Rebel Rules: Daring To Be Yourself in Business, by Chip Conley (New York: Fireside/Simon & Schuster, Inc., 2001).

Reengineering the Corporation: A Manifesto for Business Revolution, by Michael Hammer and James Champy (New York: HarperCollins Publishers, 1993).

Sam Walton: Made in America: My Story, by Sam Walton with John Huey (New York: Bantam Books, 1992).

The Seven Habits of Highly Effective People: Restoring the Character Ethic, by Stephen R. Covey (New York: Fireside/Simon & Schuster, 1989).

The Seven Spiritual Laws of Success: A Practical Guide to the Fulfillment of Your Dreams, by Deepak Chopra (San Rafael, CA: Amber-Allen Publishing, 1994).

The Soul of Success: Inspiring Quotations for Entrepreneurs, by Janet Cheatham Bell (New York: John Wiley & Sons, Inc., 1997).

A Spiritual Audit of Corporate America: A Hard Look at Spirituality, Religion and Values in the Workplace, by Ian I. Mitroff & Elzabeth A. Denton (Sam Francisco: Jossey-Bass Publishers, Inc, 1999).

The Tom Peters Seminar: Crazy Times Call for Crazy Organizations, by Tom Peters (New York: Vintage Books [a division of Random House], 1994).

22 *Immutable Laws of Branding: How to Build a Product or Service Into a World-Class Brand,* by Al Ries and Laura Reis (New York: HarperCollins, 1998).

Your Heart's Desire: Instructions for Creating the Life You Really Want, by Sonia Choquette (New York: Crown Publishing, 1997).

Women Entrepreneurs Only: 12 Women Entrepreneurs Tell the Stories of Their Success, by Gregory K. Ericksen, Ernst & Young LLP (New York: John Wiley & Sons, Inc, 1999).

ACKNOWLEDGMENTS

SO MANY PEOPLE contributed to the creation of this book, generously offering their stories, insights, and positive energy. For Cori Lathan, Jen Shiman, Kevin Gay, Lisa Rossi Dooley, Bruce Razniewski, Carolyn Carstens, Amy Weiler, Joe Bardetti, Bob Cosgrove, Jim Trompeter, Doug Wood, Orlagh Daly, Ashlee Peterson, Lauren Woodward, Inger Larsen, Cindy Hirschfeld, Amy Forstadt, Lisa Coleman, Cindy Griebler, Kim Maloney, Geordie Hrdlicka, Michelle Spiliotes, Rachel Kirk, Eric Grouse, Katie Grouse, Judy Fontana, Arthur Herbst, Jr., Nancy Desmond, Kurth Anderson, Marc Davidson, Mike Harrigan, Brad Drew, and Neela Bindu . . . Thank you for being a part of this, for all that we've shared and for everything you've taught me.

Special thanks must also go to:

My amazing editor, the hardest working man in publishing, Matthew Lore—thank God for Matthew—for patiently, kindly, and wisely guiding me through this journey. He was always right.

Christine Morin and Susan Schulman at Susan Schulman, A Literary Agency, for all their help and hard work.

Jennifer O'Connell for suggesting the title and offering invaluable input in so many areas.

Lisa Holmes and Ella Leya, my wonderful clients, colleagues, and—most of all—friends, who not only allowed me to share their stories but who also read every single draft of the manuscript for this book and gave me lots of constructive feedback, encouragement, and inspiration throughout the process.

And, last but not least, to my extraordinary family, Roger Bulger, Ruth Bulger, Faith Weiss, Michael Weiss, Arthur Herbst, Sr., and Lee Herbst, for their love, patience, generosity, and support.

Select Associates and Clients

Joe Bardetti
www.bardetti.com

Bob Cosgrove
Robert Cosgrove Design

Lisa Rossi Dooley
Sedgwick & Associates

Kevin Gay
Morningstar Theater Company

Lisa Holmes
Whimsy City
www.WhimsyCity.com

Cori Lathan
Anthrotronix
www.anthrotronix.com

Ella Leya
B-Elite
www.b-elitemusic.com

Jennifer O'Connell
Market Strategy Partners

Ashlee Peterson
www.dogsobey.com

Bruce Razniewski
Tall Tree Productions, Ltd.
www.talltree.tv

Jennifer Shiman
Angry Alien Productions
www.angryalien.com

Cyndi Simon & Lisa Coleman
The Encore Group, Inc.
www.encorestaffing.com

Jim Trompeter
Earthborne Music
www.earthbornemusic.com